'Follow the Master'

A History of Heanor Grammar School

1893 – 1976

Robert M. Mee

Heanor and District Local History Society

www.HeanorHistory.org.uk

First published 2008 by the Heanor and District Local History Society

Heanor and District Local History Society, Publication No. 8, 2008
ISBN 978 0950843 05 6

The right of Robert M. Mee to be identified as the author of this work has been asserted by him in accordance with the Copyright, Designs and Patents Act 1988.

© Copyright 2008

All rights reserved. No part of this publication may be reproduced, stored in or introduced into a retrieval system, or transmitted, in any form, or by means (electronic, mechanical, photocopying, recording or otherwise) without the prior written permission of the Heanor and District Local History Society. Any person who does any unauthorised act in relation to this publication may be liable to criminal prosecution and civil claims for damages.

Also available from the Society:
> *Two Centuries of Transport in the Heanor Area*   £3.00
> *A History of Mining in the Heanor Area*   £6.00
> *A Portrait of Heanor and District 1900 – 2004*   £7.50

Copies of all the Society's publications may be obtained from the Heanor and District Local History Society, c/o 33 Brook Street, Loscoe, Heanor, Derbyshire, DE75 7LP. (Please ensure that sufficient is added to cover postage).
Alternatively, the Society can be contacted at *mail@heanorhistory.org.uk*

Society meetings are held at the Wilmot Street Centre, Heanor, on the second Tuesday of each month from September to May at 7.30pm.

The Heanor and District Local History Society is a registered charity, no. 1006799

Printed by:

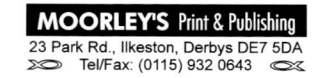

MOORLEY'S Print & Publishing
23 Park Rd., Ilkeston, Derbys DE7 5DA
Tel/Fax: (0115) 932 0643

'Follow the Master'
A History of Heanor Grammar School

Table of Contents

Acknowledgements..i

Preface...v

1. Heanor and Early Education..1

2. Heanor Technical School – the Early Years 11

3. A New Century 23

4. The New School...31

5. War and Politics: 1910 – 1919 45

6. Stoddard's Last Years – the 1920s...61

7. The 1930s and the War Years 75

8. Heanor Grammar School: 1945 – 1957 89

9. Expansion and Preparation for Change: 1957 – 1964...............105

10. The Leicestershire Model: 1964 – 1973 119

11. The Final Reorganisation: 1973 – 1976 131

12. The Legacy 141

Appendix: Roll of Honour 147

Acknowledgements

As stated in the preface to this book, the earlier incomplete work on the history of the School by **Geoffrey Stone**, the last Headmaster, has been an invaluable tool in writing much of this book. Geoffrey has taken an active role in supporting and advising throughout the long process of writing. I have argued with him that he should have joint credit for the book, but he has refused to take this. I know that he deserves it!

Numerous items in this book are reproduced by permission from original documents in the **Derbyshire Record Office**, Matlock, Derbyshire, DE4 3AG. My thanks go to **Dr Margaret O'Sullivan**, the County and Diocesan Archivist, and her staff, for their kind and able assistance. The items quoted from are the governors' minutes (D1040 C/E 20 and D1631 C/E 3/21) and a large collection of documents from the School itself (D1635).

Another major source of information has been the **Ripley and Heanor News**, and I thank the editor for their kind permission to quote from numerous articles over the years. I also thank the **Guardian** and the **Derby Evening Telegraph** for permission to quote from articles, and, in the latter case, to reproduce a photograph.

The **Heanor & District Local History Society**, of which group I am proud to be treasurer and webmaster, has not only provided the financial support to publish this book, but has also supplied 40 years of information to assist. I would particularly thank **Brian Key**, for his support with finding photographs, proofreading, and advice on publication.

I must, of course, thank the current team of the **Old Students' Association**, and especially **Ken Hopkins** – firstly for cajoling me to write the book, and secondly for their assistance in locating photographs and supplying copies of the School Magazine.

During this project I have had an unbelievable amount of help from a few individuals:

> Particular thanks must go to **John Savage**, a former pupil, who has spent a vast amount of time scouring newspapers on microfiche – without his work, this book would have been very different.
>
> Similarly, **Sheila Randall,** the last school secretary, who is now involved in the school reunions and the Heanorian Magazine, spent many hours researching documents at the record office and indexed all the school magazines. Sheila has been there with support and encouragement, especially when things weren't going well.
>
> I would also like to thank **Gillian Hall**, who does not have any link with the school, and **Sue Hardman**, a former pupil, both of whom have assisted in tracking down newspaper stories or the answers to a number of specific queries.
>
> I must also thank my wife, **Jill Mee**, not only for putting up with me during the writing of this book, but also for helping in the final stages of proofreading.

An early draft copy of another unpublished work from the 1960s by **Pam Carter** has also been of considerable help in pulling together some strands of information. And a dissertation by **Leonard Fowkes** has been used in examining early education in Heanor, with his permission, for which I am grateful.

Thanks for individual items must also go to a number of people: **Kate Pattinson** for the Bissill pictures, **Diane and Lucie Cheshire** for the Holbrook autograph book, **Roger Hull** for several school magazines, **Elizabeth Fletcher** and **Rene Copestake** for a number of school photographs, and **Andrew Knighton** for various old postcards of the school.

Books which have proved useful to this work have included **Mary and John Sheppard**'s *Aldercar – The Story of a School*, **Marion Johnson**'s *Derbyshire Village Schools*, and **Narvel Annable**'s *Heanor Schooldays – A Social History*.

I am also grateful to the Principal and staff of **South East Derbyshire College** for allowing me access to the premises. Likewise I thank **the Heanor Gate Science College** for their assistance.

If I have missed anyone out, this is not intentional. Finally, I would like to apologise to any owners of copyright material in this book if, despite my best efforts, I have not been able to locate them. If you believe that any rights that are yours have inadvertently been infringed, I would ask you to contact me and to accept my apologies.

No private profit will be made from the sale of this book - all proceeds will go to the Heanor & District Local History Society, a registered charity.

Preface

The final edition of the school magazine, aptly entitled *The Last Heanorian*, published in 1974, promised its readers that a history of the School was in preparation and would be released in 1976. Now, thirty two years later, the Heanor and District Local History Society, working in conjunction with the School's Old Students' Association, is pleased to honour that promise.

There is no criticism intended in relation to the non-appearance of any earlier work. Best laid plans do not always come to fruition. However, a huge amount of work was carried out in the 1970s in preparation for the history, primarily by the last Headmaster, Geoffrey Stone. All of Mr Stone's work on this project has been made available, together with other items he has worked on. While other acknowledgements are made elsewhere, without Geoffrey Stone's initial work, this current book would never have happened.

Heanor Grammar School, as it is normally known, despite several name changes, existed for only 83 years, from 1893 to 1976. In this short time, the school developed an enviable record in the area, achieving excellent academic records, and setting many 'firsts'. The aim of this book is to give a fairly detailed view of the history of the School from birth till its closure. Research into the history has not always been easy – minutes of meetings frequently do not tell the whole story, nor do newspaper articles of the time.

It is inevitable there will be errors and omissions in this publication. I am sure that as soon as we have committed to print, I shall discover something materially incorrect. I can only apologise for this, and claim that, at the time of writing, everything is committed to the best of my knowledge. I would be grateful to any reader who can add to or correct anything within the book. Any mistakes in the publication are unintentional, but I bear full responsibility for them.

The subtitle of this book is *A History of Heanor Grammar School*. A lot of discussion has taken place over whether to use the definite article rather than the indefinite. My view is that if ten people all set out at the same time to write 'the' history of the School, they would all end up with a different end result, albeit with the same main points. For this reason alone, mine is definitely 'A History'. In particular, this book is a history of the institution, and not, as is the case with many similar publications, a record of pupils' recollections – I hope you will bear that in mind if it is not what you expected.

Readers will discover that there is far more in this book about some periods than others. There is much better documentation for the first forty years, and the last twenty years. I would like to have included much more about the School during the Second World War and the periods either side of it, but this has been more difficult to obtain. I hope that what is presented is an accurate reflection of what was going on at the time.

John Bunyan's poem, turned into the hymn *To be a Pilgrim*, was selected as the School Hymn, certainly no later than 1938. It is apt that the title of this book should quote from what became, for those of us who attended the School, totally engraved in our memories.

> *He who would valiant be, 'gainst all disaster*
> *Let him in constancy follow the Master*
> *There's no discouragement shall make him once relent*
> *His first avowed intent to be a pilgrim.*

I was one of the last pupils at Heanor Grammar School, leaving in 1975. I may not have thought so at the time, but, in retrospect, I was proud to *'follow the Master'*.

Robert Mee
April 2008

Chapter 1

Heanor and Early Education

When it was founded in 1893, the secondary school at Heanor was the first maintained mixed secondary school in the county to be financed out of a local rate, and may perhaps have been the first in the whole country. Its origins and its history are therefore of interest, not only to old students and people living in the area, but also to the wider public.

But before we can look at the history of a single institution, we need to understand the community in which that school was formed, to view the 'wider picture'.

In his *Review of the Early History of Heanor Grammar School*, the first Headmaster, Ralph Stoddard, presented a rather idyllic view of Heanor's past:

> *Heanor is of Ancient Days.*
>
> *Once upon a time it was just a small village built about an old Saxon Church on the summit of the hill. Later on, there was an early Norman Church together with a vicarage, a school, an Olde Hall, the village stocks, a tithe barn, farms, cottages, the countryside, fresh air and the people.*
>
> *The vicarage occupied the site of the present Conservative Club, whilst fifty yards or so away from the Vicarage, on the Ilkeston Road, was the great seat of Learning, a very tiny, one roomed school, recently demolished.*
>
> *On the left of the main entrance to the Church Yard, stood the 'Olde Hall' of which the foundations are still in evidence. It was a fair specimen of a half-timbered English homestead in the days of the Tudors.*
>
> *The Village stocks were in a very handy position, on the edge of the highway near the present Heanor Town Hall, whilst the Tithe Barn was also there or thereabouts, with Malt Rooms adjoining.*
>
> *Two or three hundred years ago, the second Heanor Hall was built.*

Whilst there is nothing in Mr Stoddard's account which is not believed to be correct, he only tells half the story.

Heanor, meaning 'high ridge', is one of a series of hilltop villages which look down on the Erewash Valley, the border between Derbyshire and Nottinghamshire. At the top of the hill, standing at about 400 feet above sea level, there has been a church since Saxon times. There is some evidence of Roman activity in the area, for a horde of coins was found at nearby Shipley. There is even evidence of occupation in the neolithic period.

With the coming of the Normans, *'Hainoure'* is mentioned in the Domesday Book as being the held by Warner, under William Peveril; Warner held six manors within four villages, namely Heanor, Codnor, Langley and 'Smithycote'. So Mr Stoddard was right, *'Heanor is of Ancient Days'*.

The manor passed to the de Greys, who built a stronghold at Codnor, and occupied the castle from the thirteenth to the end of the fifteenth century. Under the de Greys a new church was built, on the same site as its Saxon predecessor. All that remains of the old church now is the tower, dating back to the 15th century. The rest of the church was rebuilt in 1868, and again in 1982. Even less remains of Codnor Castle today.

The de Greys of Codnor were followed by the Zouche family, and then the Masters, until the estate was finally sold, in 1862, to the Butterley Company.

Whilst the principal families in the area were the Lords of the Manor, the centuries after the Norman Conquest saw a number of other large houses develop. At Shipley, which was also mentioned in the Domesday Book, the Leche family, and then the Mundys built and enlarged Shipley Hall. At Smalley, there were Smalley Hall and Stainsby Hall. And at Heanor there was Heanor Hall, what Mr Stoddard calls the *'Olde Hall'*. This was probably built in the early 1600s, and was home to the Roper family.

Mr Stoddard is correct about the location of the vicarage and the tithe barn, along with the malt-rooms. The original Heanor Hall was possibly as described, and in front of it stood an inn, the 'King of Prussia' (now the 'Market Hotel').

What is omitted, though, from the description, is what was, by the end of the nineteenth century, the life-blood of the Heanor area: mining and industry.

While the rural nature of some of the area cannot be forgotten, nobody reading Mr Stoddard's piece would have needed reminding whence Heanor's money came.

Coal mining has been going on in the area since at least the thirteenth century. It was mainly the existence of rich coal seams which led to the development of extensive transport links to the area: first with turnpike roads, then the canals at Langley Mill, and finally the railways. Having improved transport, together with a ready supply of energy, meant that other industries were quick to follow, and, with that, there was a rapid growth in population.

As early as the sixteenth century, Sir John Zouche of Codnor Castle had built iron furnaces at Loscoe, using local coal and water from Loscoe Dam. From the eighteenth century onwards, the town saw the rapid growth of its coal mines, along with hosiery, engineering and, later, pottery industries. Their development rapidly, and completely, altered the character of Heanor, turning it into a typical small mining and industrial town, albeit set in rural surroundings. The *'countryside'*, referred to by Mr Stoddard, along with its *'fresh air'*, was now being filled with a clutter of streets with their terraced houses to accommodate the workforce.

Hosiery grew up in the town as a cottage industry, with framework knitters working at home. In due course, factories such as Morley's and Fletcher's were built, although a good deal of work was still done by hand at home. Down in the valley at Langley Mill, where the transport links were closest, heavier industry, particularly Turner's ironworks, developed.

But coal still provided the main income source for the great houses of the area, most notably at Shipley Hall. And it was the coal industry which paid for the second Heanor Hall. The Hall, a Georgian building, was built sometime in the eighteenth century, and was occupied by the Fletcher family, owners of coal mines in the Heanor and Loscoe areas. At the end of the century, it was sold to John Sutton, another major mine owner. When Mr Sutton died, his wife's niece and her husband, Mr John Ray, came to live with Mrs Sutton at the Hall, and subsequently inherited it. Mr Ray died in 1867, and in 1881 Heanor Hall was bought by Mr Alfred Edward Miller Mundy, of Shipley Hall, for £9,653/18s/6d.

Originally, the Hall had large grounds which incorporated much of what is now the town centre. From the vicarage, a high wall ran all the way down Market Street as far as Red Lion Square, enclosing the Hall's grounds. Between Heanor Hall and Shipley Hall there was little besides open fields (and the Sye Lane pit). However, following the purchase of the estate by the Mundy family, it began to be broken up and developed. By 1890 Mundy Street, and the other streets in the town centre were being opened as thoroughfares, and building plots were being sold for housing and shops. Part of the estate was used to lay out the Market Place in 1894. Prior to this development of what is now the town centre, most of the settlement had been further down the hill, off High Street, and along Derby Road, 'Tag Hill'.

It can be seen, therefore, that Heanor, as a town, was populated by workers. There were a few relatively wealthy families, those who owned the mines, factories or land, and a few middle-class tradesmen. But the vast majority of the population were poor miners and factory workers. As their families came along, for most of them the prime aim was to get the children to work as soon as they could.

However, unlike many similar towns, Heanor had a fine tradition of 'self-improvement', led by the few relatively well-off inhabitants, and by the church and the chapels. Comparatively early, for example, Heanor had a piped water supply, and likewise gas was laid on, from the town's own gasworks, as early as 1855. This characteristic of self-improvement is evident when we look at the development of education in the area.

Educational provision in the Heanor area prior to the Education Act of 1870 was, as elsewhere, rather piecemeal. Heanor itself had no formal school at all until 1848, and any education that was provided for the children of the town was carried out in a number of privately run 'academies', alongside church or chapel schools. As early as 1830, Jesse Meykin and Thomas Roscoe were shown in county directories as running schools in the town. These were, of course, fee-paying, and few parents in the Heanor area would be able to afford the cost. But over the next 60 years, there was a steady increase in these private schools, followed by a sharp decline as publicly owned schools gained in stature.

The earliest formal schools were those funded by charities. The oldest in the immediate area, built in 1664, was at West Hallam, established from a bequest made by the Rev. John Scargill two years earlier. A little closer, and more relevant to this history, is the Richardson Endowed School for Boys at Smalley. The School was founded in 1721 under the terms of the wills of John and Samuel Richardson; lands purchased were to provide a school and pay a quarterly pension for 12 *'poor boys'*, six from Smalley, three from Horsley Woodhouse, and three from Heanor.

The first school of the Victorian age in the area was at Shipley, where the squires of Shipley Hall, the Mundys, had built a schoolroom in 1842. By 1846 it had around 60 pupils, a number which rose to 180 by 1857. The school was *'supported by subscriptions, and a small weekly payment from the children'*.

The impetus for education to change from being at the largess of individual benefactors, as at Smalley and Shipley, started in 1833 when Parliament allocated a sum of £20,000 to support the development of schools *'for the education of the children of the poorer classes in Great Britain'*. This money was divided equally between two denominational bodies, the British and Foreign Schools Society, which was non-conformist, and the National Society for Promoting the Education of the Poor in the Principles of the Church of England (normally referred to as the National Society). Both these organisations worked with local groups who wished to raise funds and provide schools.

One of the oldest of the local National Schools, Crosshill School was opened in 1844.

Church-sponsored education was provided certainly as early as 1840 in the Church Institute on Sye Lane (Ilkeston Road), a single-roomed building which held around 40 boys, and which Mr Stoddard referred to as *'the great seat of learning'*. But it was not until 1848 that the first National School was built in Heanor, on High Street where the Job Centre now stands. The grant to cover the cost of building the school was provided by the National Society, but the running costs were met by local donations, assistance from the church, and pupil fees. Codnor also had two early National Schools, at Crosshill (1844), alongside the church, and on Jessop Street.

The non-conformists were also running schools, but not generally in buildings which would survive as schools. The Wesleyans opened a day school at Heanor in 1849, where there was a sliding scale of fees: those who could afford to do so were expected to pay one shilling a week, while poor children were admitted for a penny a week. The Baptists at Loscoe built a school on Furnace Lane in 1858, which had over 200 pupils initially, at a cost of one penny a week (the schoolroom still exists).

In 1870 the Education Act introduced the concept of compulsory education, but not the reality. The Act also set a maximum school fee of 9d a week, a clear indication that it was aimed at the education of poor children; the middle-classes, still using private schools, would already be paying far more than that. The aim was that every child should have the possibility of attending an elementary school. However, whether or not attendance would be compulsory was, for the first few years, a matter for the locality, not the government.

Under the Act, a count of school places currently available in each area had to be undertaken. If there were insufficient places provided by the voluntary bodies, then a School Board would have to be elected, and they would have the power to raise funds by a rate in order to pay for new schools. The previous provision in Heanor meant that no School Board was required in the town. The Act also continued to encourage the growth of voluntary schools, increasing the finance available to them.

In 1876, a further Act placed a duty on the parents of all children under 14 years to ensure that they received *'efficient instruction in reading, writing and arithmetic'*. Employment of those under the age of ten was not allowed, and between the ages of 10 and 13 children needed a certificate issued by a school inspector before they could work. Compulsory attendance at school from the age of five to ten was finally introduced in 1880 (rising to the age of 11 in 1893).

The period of school expansion in Heanor coincided with a long dynasty of rectors at the Church of St. Lawrence. The rector of Heanor from 1866 to 1879 was the Rev. Frederick Corfield, who was followed by his three sons: Conyngham W.G. Corfield (1879 to 1886), Claud E.L. Corfield (1886 to 1911), and Ashley T. Corfield (1911 to 1917). The Corfields generally, and Claud Corfield in particular, were, in conjunction with the National Society, responsible for the wide-scale development of church-funded elementary schools in the parish of Heanor.

In Frederick Corfield's day, Laceyfields Road School at Langley, for girls and infants was built in 1871. In Langley Mill, the boys' school on Station Road (1872), and the school for girls and infants on Cromford Road, Aldercar (1875), were both funded by the Butterley Company, with support from the church.

Two members of the Corfield family. Claud (on the left), with his brother Ashley. The photograph is dated 1911, after Claud Corfield had moved to Taunton.

In the twenty years after the arrival of Claud Corfield school building went from strength to strength. Mundy Street School, Heanor, was opened in 1891 and enlarged in 1893 and Canon Corfield personally funded the building of the school on East Street at Marlpool in 1892. The Commonside School (later renamed Corfield School) on Thorpes Road was built for girls and infants in 1902. Elnor Street infants' school (1896), and a girls' school at Sedgwick Street (1909), completed the picture for Langley Mill.

Mundy Street Boys' School: opened in 1891, closed 2005.

Rev. Claud Corfield was the chairman of the managing committee at almost all of Heanor's schools, and his face is perhaps the most easily recognised in old school group photographs of the early twentieth century.

Other schools were added in the area, which were either not in the parish of Heanor, or were not the result of the Corfields' work: the infants' school on Mill Lane, Codnor (1872) was funded by the Methodists, while the school on Loscoe Denby Lane (1895) was provided by the Church of England. Later additions were the boys' school on Claramount Road at Langley (1908), the Council (later Howitt) Schools on Loscoe Road (1915), and the Codnor Central Council School (1912).

The denominational provision of elementary education in the Heanor area worked well, as is shown by the lack of a local school board. The schools were also of a high standard. Bulmer's Directory, in 1895, describing the town, states:

> *The school premises and the instruction given are fully up to the requirements of the government, and in the results obtained, these schools rank among the best in the country.*

As stated earlier, the first public denominational schools were targeted almost exclusively at the poor. However, as they became more established and the number of places grew, the use of private schools by the relatively few middle-class families of the Heanor area diminished. The number of such schools had grown quite significantly throughout the nineteenth century, and some of them were run from quite imposing addresses. For example, during the 1880s, Aldercar Hall, the former home of the Wright family of the Butterley Company, was used for a few years as a boarding school by Mr Frank Adams.

By 1890, a directory showed no less than six private schools in the area. Miss Minnie Bramley had a day school on Church Street, while Miss Sarah Anne Clarke had another in West Valley (the bottom of Market Street). Mr Hodgson Grassby ran an Academy on Ray Street, while Miss Clara Jane Parkins and Miss Sarah Anne Redgate both had schools on West Hill. The final one was a 'School for Young Ladies', held at Heanor Hall, the proprietors being Miss Kate Linsey and Fraulein Ursina Fopp, from Switzerland. An autograph book, apparently owned by Miss Clara Holbrook (after whom Claramount Road is named), daughter of the town surveyor, contains the signatures of both proprietors of the school, along with several other females of Swiss nationality who indicate that they were at Heanor Hall at the time. The Heanor Hall signatures are dated between 1891 and 1893. Other signatures are from members of several other well known families of the area. This suggests the type of person who might have been using the School for Young Ladies at this time – perhaps a Heanor version of a 'finishing school'?

The autographs of Ursina Fopp and Kate Linsey, at Heanor Hall, April 1893, from Clara Holbrook's autograph book.

However, the number of private schools in the town, as far as the trade directories were concerned, dropped back down to just two in 1895, compared to the six in 1890.

None of this has any direct part in the history of Heanor Grammar School, but is given to show the developing picture of education in the area. It was about to develop far more….

Chapter 2

Heanor Technical School – the Early Years

Whilst elementary education was becoming firmly established in the 1870s and 1880s, there was little provision, as we have seen, for anything beyond that. Children had to attend school until the age of ten, and could not start work before the age of 13 unless a school inspector certified that they could read, write, and do arithmetic. Since the wealthy could continue education, it is not surprising that a demand grew for a higher level of education to be made available for others.

The Technical Instruction Act of 1889 gave powers to the newly created County and County Borough Councils to enable them to meet demands for secondary education. Derbyshire County Council subsequently indicated its intention of assisting in the establishment of District Technical Schools, and appointed a Technical Education Committee for the purpose.

It was with this background that, in 1893, the Heanor Local Board appointed a 'Heanor Technical Education Committee' under the chairmanship of Mr Thomas Mayfield.

At this time, there was no provision for secondary education in the 375 square miles extending from Clay Cross in the north to Long Eaton in the south. With the transport links already available to Heanor, the town seemed an ideal location for a district technical school. There were four railway stations within walking distance of the town centre:

    Heanor Northern station (1891), on the branch line from Ilkeston;
    Heanor Midland station (1890), with trains from Ripley;
    Langley Mill station (1847), on the Erewash Valley line, giving access from Clay Cross and Alfreton in the north and from Long Eaton and Ilkeston in the south; and
    Langley Mill and Eastwood station (1875), with trains from Pinxton and Kimberley.

The early and profuse provision of railways in the area would give pupils easy access to any new facility, and this factor cannot be underestimated. It would not be until 1913, with the laying of a tram route from Ripley to Nottingham, passing directly through Heanor, that any easy alternative means of transport would become available.

The town's Technical Education Committee obtained support from the County Council to assist them in starting a 'district technical school' and 'organised science school' under the government Science and Art Department. On the Committee were prominent figures, like Mr A.E. Miller Mundy, Mr FitzHerbert Wright, Rev. Claud E.L. Corfield, Mr S. Pender, and Mr F. Cattle, clerk to the Local Board. It also included County Council representation. Various options were examined to improve the provision of technical education in the area. Then, in March 1893 it was heard that the current occupants of Heanor Hall (presumably the girls' school, since Miss Linsey and Fraulein Fopp did not sign the autograph book until April 1893) were to give it up. The Committee approached Mr Mundy's steward, and was informed that the Hall would be available if they required it.

Heanor Hall, shortly after becoming the Technical School.

The option of a single large school in Heanor was preferred; the Hall required little alteration - £20 would cover it - and the plan did not rely on the purchase of a new building. The Committee requested a 21 years lease on the Heanor Hall, but Mr Mundy was only prepared to offer the Hall for 14 years (until 1907), with the option of taking possession of any of the cowsheds, etc., to the north of the Hall with only six months notice. There were some objections from Langley Mill committee members, who wanted a dedicated building for their own technical education, and a smaller site than Heanor Hall in Heanor itself. But the plans went ahead, and were approved by the County Technical Education Committee. The County promised to meet one-third of the initial outlay costs and to provide forty free scholarships, to include both school fees and railway-fare, to be distributed among the elementary schools of the district. (The 'district' was to cover the whole area previously mentioned, from Clay Cross to Long Eaton.)

This, however, covered only part of the initial expenses of starting the School and only a small proportion of the running costs. Consequently, an appeal for voluntary subscriptions had to be launched covering the whole area to be served. Additionally, four members of the Committee, Mr T. Mayfield, the chairman, Mr J. Holbrook, Mr J. Holmes and Mr S. Towson, jointly guaranteed to the Heanor Joint Stock Bank the not inconsiderable sum for those days of £2,000. Their altruism and courage were not in vain, for they were never called upon to meet their guarantees.

With this encouragement, the Committee proceeded to appoint a headmaster for the School in June 1893. Out of around 40 applicants, they chose Ralph Stoddard, BSc, from the People's College, Nottingham. Mr Stoddard went on to serve the School for the next 35 years until his retirement in 1928.

The hand-written Memorandum of Agreement drawn up between the committee and Mr Stoddard is still in existence.

> *Memorandum of Agreement made the First day of November One thousand eight hundred and ninety three between Thomas Mayfield of Heanor in the County of Derby Factory Manager John Holbrook of Heanor aforesaid Surveyor John Holmes of Heanor aforesaid gentleman and Samuel Towson of Langley Mill in the parish of Heanor aforesaid Joiner (for and on behalf of themselves and the other members of the Heanor Technical Education Committee) of the one part and Ralph Stoddard of Heanor aforesaid Schoolmaster of the other part. Whereby it is agreed between the said parties hereto as follows:-*
>
> *1) The said Ralph Stoddard shall conduct the Heanor District Technical School and teach the scholars for the time being attending there from*

> the nineteenth day of September One thousand eight hundred and ninety three in accordance with the requirements of the Science and Art Department, the Technical Education Committee of the Derbyshire County Council and the Heanor Technical Education Committee.
>
> 2) The said Thomas Mayfield John Holbrook John Holmes and Samuel Towson shall pay to the said Ralph Stoddard for his services as Head Master of the said School the sum of One hundred and eighty pounds a year payable by equal monthly instalments on the eighteenth day of every month.
>
> 3) The holidays of the said School shall be two weeks at Christmas One week at Easter and Six weeks at Midsummer in each year.
>
> 4) This Agreement may be terminated at any time by either party giving to the other three calendar months notice in writing. Such proportion of the said Salary as is due on the expiration of the said notice shall be paid accordingly.

The five parties to the agreement were joined by a sixth signature, that of Hodgson Grassby, the proprietor of the academy on Ray Street, who was now to become the secretary to the School.

One of Mr Stoddard's first duties on arriving in Heanor was to issue a leaflet appeal to the 100,000 or so inhabitants of the district which the School was intended to serve, seeking donations for funds to pay for set-up expenses as well as helping with the ongoing staff costs, etc. Whilst the Heanor Local Board were contributing a 1d rate, this only just covered the rent of Heanor Hall (at £106 a year). Fees for pupils were approximately £2 per pupil; the County Council were providing scholarships for 40 pupils, and the Richardson Charity of Smalley provided eight others from 1898, the remaining pupils paid their own fees at 13/- per term.

Besides fund raising, Mr Stoddard also had the task of preparing the building to become a school – and he only had six weeks in which to do it. Rooms inside the hall were adapted and laid out, and much of the furniture (desks, laboratory tables, cupboards, blackboards, and easels) had to be made from scratch.

There was no official opening of the Heanor Technical School in September 1893. Mr Stoddard arrived to open the front door and walked in quietly with the first of the pupils.

The new School was notable in several ways. It was the first secondary school in the county to be co-educational; it was the first secondary school to be maintained, in part, by the product of a 'penny technical rate' levied by an Urban District Committee; and it was the first maintained secondary school in the county outside the major towns of Derby and Chesterfield (although, of course, there were several old-established endowed grammar schools as, for instance, at Dronfield, Staveley and Ashbourne). Indeed, it has been claimed that it was the first co-educational maintained secondary school in the whole country. Whether this is true or not, the School must certainly have been among the first of its kind.

According to a report of 1904, the start of the first academic year in 1893 saw a total of 28 pupils at the new school. By the end of that year, the numbers had risen to 90. And for most of that year Mr Stoddard appears to have been the only full-time member of teaching staff. In June 1894, towards the end of the first academic year, the School appointed its first mistress, Miss Athya, from Liverpool, who primarily taught French. At the start of the new autumn term, in September 1894, they were joined by Mr W.T. Clarke, as second master, and he took over most of the teaching of mathematics and science. Mr Clarke was to remain at the School 21 years; he was the grandfather of the future Home Secretary (2004-2006), Charles Clarke. Another early teacher, who joined the School in 1898 and stayed for over thirty years, was the flamboyant William Rodway

William Rodway Barnes, art master from 1898 to 1932.

Barnes, the art master; he had previously served as a mounted policeman under Cecil Rhodes in South Africa, and, as well as painting, his hobby was collecting swords, sabres, claymores and dirks.

The precise curriculum is not recorded for the early years, but, as Mr Stoddard recollected, '*Science was necessarily the chief target for the day. But English, Geography, History, French, Needlework, Woodwork, Clay-modelling, Cookery, Art and the Violin were not entirely forgotten.*' We know from examination results that science in this context included mathematics, physics, and both theoretical and practical chemistry. This was quite a remarkable performance by a staff of only three full-time and three or four part-time teachers.

And the staff were teaching others besides the School's day pupils. The Technical Education Committee had, for a number of years, offered evening 'continuation classes'. An announcement in the Ripley and Heanor News on 15 September 1893 listed subjects such as '*letter-writing, accounts-keeping, reading, composition, arithmetic, euclid, singing by note, French, history, duties of the citizen* [so citizenship classes are not so new!], *cooking, etc*'. With the opening of the new school, further technical subjects were now added to the prospectus. Subjects seen in contemporary reports include the following (and, where known, the enrolment statistics for 1894/5): sick-nursing, Pitman shorthand, mining (22), geometry (9), physiography, magnetism and electricity (14), applied mechanics (9), machine construction (15), freehand drawing (46), chemistry (20), and practical chemistry (13).

Although 40 years later there might be a great deal of difference between the School and later Mining College, the early days of the School show a clear emphasis on the technical nature of the subjects offered. The scientific subjects were generally taught by Mr Stoddard, the engineering subjects by Mr Bardill, and nursing by Mrs Cooke. Additionally, even in the first year, the School provided a well-stocked public library, of which Mr Grassby was the administrator.

The Annual Report of the Technical Committee of the Department of Secondary Education of the Derbyshire County Council for the year 1894 gave an interesting account of the School in its earliest form:

Heanor Hall School – entered upon its second year of work in 1894. An additional master was appointed, making the staff to consist of two masters and one mistress. The numbers went up from 90 to 120, being a net increase of 30 in the twelve months. The suddenness with which this school has grown and taken the leading place as the largest Secondary School in the County is very remarkable. It can, however, hardly be compared with the grammar schools, since its fees are much lower, and, while it draws from all sections of the middle classes, it contains far more scholars from the homes of small tradesmen and intelligent artisans. Its curriculum is more scientific and commercial than that of the ordinary grammar school, and corresponds in fact with that of a German Realschule, which is mainly designed for the training of those who may expect to occupy the position of foremen and similar positions of subordinate control. They do not, however, send pupils only in that direction, but cover a much wider area of industrial and commercial life. Whenever Heanor Hall School has been inspected, its proceedings have always given an impression of liveliness and smartness, from which the best results must follow. In the examinations and inspections of the Science and Art Department excellent results have been obtained, and it is largely by the grant earned that the school is supported. Under the new scheme of that department for Organised Science Schools, there is no doubt that still better educational results will follow, without detriment to the financial status of the school. The attendance is remarkably regular. The scholars seem in sympathy with the teachers. Excellent order is maintained. The teaching methods are correct, but upon the girls' side there is not that degree of smartness and efficiency which is seen in the boys' classes. The experiment of mixed classes still continues and is found to answer, and to be free from objections. The experience gained in this direction is likely to be specially valuable in the future. The scholars in attendance completely filled the premises at the close of the Session, and the local Committee had before them the question of building additional class-rooms.

This county-wide report is interesting in that it seems to struggle with the name of the School, a theme which continued throughout its existence. While the specific entry above talks of '*Heanor Hall School*', the same document also refers to it as the '*Heanor School of Science*', '*Heanor Hall School of Science*', as well as '*Heanor Technical School*'. Elsewhere, reference has also been seen to the '*East Derbyshire Technical School*'. Heanor Technical School was the correct name, and in the early days, enrolment at the School was signified not by a uniform, but by the pupils wearing a badge *'in the shape of a silver monogram embodying the letters HTS'*. (The abbreviation 'TS' is also what gave rise to the nickname for its pupils as 'Toffee-Suckers'.)

Heanor Toffee Suckers badge.

The above report is also interesting in relation to the way in which one of the earliest mixed schools was organised, for it seems clear that some subjects were taught to mixed groups and some to single-sex groups. It is not clear whether the single-sex groups were merely for craft subjects, but the implication of the report would seem to indicate otherwise. However, even though the School was mixed from the outset, it was not until the late 1950s that both sexes were allowed to enter the School by the same entrance, or use the same staircases inside the building.

The financial resources available to the Committee responsible for running the School came from various sources, but unlike the older grammar schools of the county, there were no endowments to fall back on - the venture had to be self-sufficient from the outset.

>Firstly, there was the product of the 'penny rate', but this was only just enough to cover the rent of the premises.

>Secondly, there were the school fees. Mr Dix recalled that these were one shilling per week, with extra charges for books and sports; and elsewhere it was recorded that they were *'thirteen shillings per term to children of parishioners who pay the penny rate, twenty-one shillings per term to all others'*.

>Thirdly, the County Council provided 40 scholarships, to which were added eight scholarships provided by the Richardson Foundation of Smalley, from 1898 to 1944, and several more from the Scargill Trust of West Hallam. (County scholarships were obtained through competitive examination, with far more candidates than places available.)

Next, there was the income from the South Kensington Science and Art Examinations. Under this scheme, the sum of £2 per head was paid for pupils who succeeded in passing examinations in elementary theoretical chemistry, mathematics, physics and related subjects, and £3 per head for those who passed practical chemistry. Mr Stoddard recalled that in one year no less than sixty-one pupils passed the practical chemistry examination, so earning the School £183 on that account alone.

Finally, in a system which is no different from today, the school made its own efforts to raise funds. The first recorded summer fair was held over three days at the end of July 1894. With brass bands and dancing, temporary electrical equipment lighting up the school and its grounds, stalls and refreshments, a total of £250 was raised. This was a remarkable sum for the period, especially when compared with the Headmaster's annual salary of £180, and it indicates the strength of local support for the School at the time.

From this income, the Technical School Committee had to pay two-thirds of the salaries of the staff and the secretary (Mr H. Grassby), together with the cost of heating, lighting, cleaning, equipment and materials for woodwork, needlework, cookery and the science laboratories. The remaining third of the expenses was paid by the County Technical Education Committee. These arrangements continued until the Education Act of 1902 introduced new financial provisions for secondary schools under the newly-created Board of Education.

As previously mentioned, the pupils at the school came from a very wide area. Around 20 per cent of places were reserved for residents of the Heanor Urban District area, since it was they who paid the 1d rate. The remaining 80 per cent were listed with homes in Long Eaton, Sawley, Sandiacre, Trowell, Stanton, West Hallam, Shipley, Smalley Common, Horsley Woodhouse, Marehay, Ripley, Somercotes, Swanwick, Alfreton, Codnor Park, Ironville, Eastwood, Nuthall and Kimberley. Those who needed transport to get to school would normally catch the train and walk up the hill from Langley Mill or the Midland Road Station. One pupil, Roper from Sawley, left home daily at about 6 o'clock in the morning, travelling by horseback, and stabling his horse in the former stables of the Hall.

And so, in a very short period after it had opened, the school was already fully used. From 90 pupils in 1893, the numbers rose to over 130 by the turn of the century; they would rise further to around 350 by 1908, until changes in the catchment area caused them to become a little more manageable.

However, it is clear that little, if any, structural work was done to adapt Heanor Hall to its new purpose as a school; it was the school that had to fit into the accommodation available. It is at this point perhaps worth obtaining a few descriptions of the building and grounds.

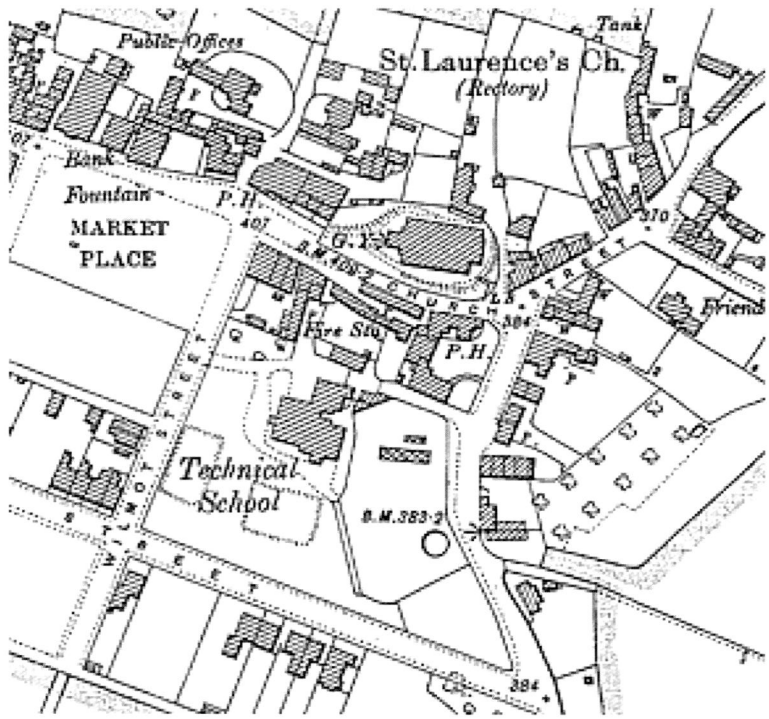

The 1901 Ordnance Survey Map, showing the site of Heanor Hall. The main drive to the Hall runs to Wilmot Street, but before the establishment of the Market Place it came out onto Market Street near the Town Hall. There was/is a rear entrance off Ilkeston Road. The public house to the north east of the Hall was the original Crown Inn, demolished in 1913.

Firstly, Mr Stoddard himself, in his 1949 *Review* describes the school in the 1900s, when even more pupils had to be catered for.

> *Some were in the 'Parlour', some were in the Kitchen, some were in the Billiard Room, always known as the Art Room, some were in the first floor upstairs rooms, some were in the Garrett* [sic]*, some were in the Garden, and when possible some were in the Chemical lab, some were in the 'Great Seat of Learning' previously referred to and known as the Church Institute, some were in the Wesleyan domain.*

The '*Garrett*' he referred to was in fact the attic, where two bedrooms had been knocked into one and equipped with benches and a lathe. It is of interest that the School already used other buildings, the Church Institute on Ilkeston Road (or Sye Lane as it was then), and the Wesleyan Schoolroom on the Market Place.

Outside were the Hall gardens, surrounded by a high wall, and Mr Stoddard went on to describe these:

> *At the back of the School, towering magnificently aloft, were giant beech trees, leading to an old-world garden, where apple trees and pears and plums abounded, and trellised vine and cucumbers and things..... There was as well a shady bower, all roofed aloft with radiant trails of Traveller's Joy, in bud and flower and fruit, and near the southern end, the 'Pond' – the pond where lilies grew and dragons lived – greenish, glistening dragon-flies....*

Another description came from H.H. Dix, who started at Heanor Technical School in 1895, writing in the school magazine in 1953:

> *There were many features which recalled its former function as Heanor Hall, the home of the Ray family. The imposing entrance, the large sash windows, and in the grounds a wonderful covered walk, known as 'The Avenue', which terminated at the Head's private entrance – a door in the wall opposite his residence in Mundy Street.* [Mundy Street itself was newly built, having been laid out in 1890. Mr Stoddard lived at a house named 'Abbey Holm'.]

And a final description, from the same edition of the magazine, was given by H.L. Harlow, who started at the School in 1905:

> *The School occupied roughly the same position as does our present school, but the main entrance was what is now the way into the Council yard* [off the Market Place], *a winding drive sweeping majestically round to the façade of what looked like a lovely old ivy-clad country residence with terraced lawns, tennis courts, flower beds and a large orchard. I should say that we could have branched left to enter at the tradesmen's entrance, past Old Turton's kitchen where eggs, or anything that you required cooking for your dinner, were deposited, or we might even have strayed into the chemistry lab, a sort of out-building, now the headquarters of the Water Department of Heanor Urban District Council. If my memory serves me correctly, above the front door was a crest, that of the Ray family, which became, and still is, our School Crest.* [Mr Harlow is not correct here – the Ray family crest was indeed above the door of Heanor Hall, but it was not the same as the school crest.] *The beautiful gardens were by now looking rather bedraggled, the lawns were grassless and were being used as football and cricket pitches, and the tree-shaded pond had become green and slimy.*

Right from the outset there was mention of sport at the school. More will follow in subsequent chapters, but the first reference to an inter-school competition was in April 1895, when the Technical School lost 2-0 in the schoolboys' football competition final against the nearby Mundy Street Boys' School. And, from a newspaper report in 1900, it is clear that the annual sports day had been instituted in 1895, taking place on the Heanor Town Ground.

In the space of a few years, Heanor Hall had developed from a country gentleman's house, via a private finishing school, into a thriving publicly funded Technical School. The problem, though, was that it was thriving so well that the building was struggling to contain it!

Chapter 3

A New Century

The new Heanor Technical School prospered from the first, and the next ten years saw steady growth and development, which taxed to the utmost the resources available. The report of the County Technical Education Committee for 1901-2 recorded that there were by then 128 pupils (98 boys and 30 girls) and that the staff consisted of Mr Stoddard, *'assisted by one graduate (BSc) and three others, with two visiting teachers'*.

Heanor Hall, around 1900, showing the junction of Mundy Street and Wilmot Street. Notice the high wall around the School at this time.

A significant change occurred with the Education Act of 1902. This led to the establishment of the Board of Education in London and County Education Committees. Locally, this meant that the main burden of financial responsibility now passed to the County Council. The School was no longer dependent on examination successes, *'payment by results'*, in order to keep going. It was now renamed the Heanor Secondary and Technical School.

Within Derbyshire, three other schools had developed, like Heanor, under the School of Science Regulations. These were at Clay Cross, Glossop and New Mills; Heanor Technical School was by far the largest of the four. In fact, by 1904 Heanor Technical School was the second largest secondary school

23

(including the old grammar schools) maintained by the County; only Lady Manners School, at Bakewell, had more pupils (146).

Throughout the earliest years of the School, there are no surviving official records, and few documents of any kind originating from the School. The first County Education Committee minutes start in 1903. It is known that there were inspections by the HMI in both 1907 and 1913, but these reports also no longer exist.

However, one document which does survive is the *Report on Secondary and Higher Education in Derbyshire*, prepared for the County Council in 1904 by Michael E. Sadler. This presented a clear and thorough picture, warts and all, of the state of the School in 1904. It is worth quoting significant portions of the report.

> *The evening classes are an important part of the institution, and at least two teachers (Mr Stoddard, the headmaster, and Mr Clarke) teach in both the day school and the evening classes. The school is stated to have been the first co-educational school of a secondary nature in the County, and the committee of the school to have been the first Urban District Committee in the County to levy the penny technical rate.*
>
> *The buildings in which the school is carried on were originally a gentleman's residence, comprising large house and grounds. These have been adapted and enlarged. The accommodation is stated to be sufficient for 150, but at the time of my inquiry there were 134 pupils present (106 boys and 28 girls) in the school, and certainly it seemed sufficiently full with that number. There are forty County Council scholarships held in the school, and seventeen other scholarships. School fees are 13s per term to children of parishioners who pay the penny rate, 21s per term for all others.*
>
> *The buildings are not adequate for the work attempted. There is no main hall. There are four class rooms, the numbers usually accommodated being 30, 45, 45, 20-27 respectively. The chemical laboratory and physical laboratory take 25 and 20 respectively. The art room is used as a class room. There is no gymnasium. There are good grounds around the school, with tennis court, and there is also a field of seven acres (a short distance away), which is rented for hockey, cricket, and football.*

The headmaster and his assistant both hold the BSc degree; the art teacher, Mr Barnes, is a gold medallist, and highly qualified for his work; Miss Birt, the senior assistant mistress, holds the Cambridge Teachers' Diploma.

The science subjects are physics and chemistry. To these, together with mathematics, about twelve hours of school time are given weekly. The drawing, on the average, receives over three hours a week for each pupil. To history and geography six hours are allotted. The amount of time given to English history and geography is, on the whole, very inadequate. Latin forms no part of the ordinary curriculum, but is taught to those who are taking a University examination. The teaching of drawing is admirable.

A hundred and sixteen out of a hundred and thirty-four pupils come from the public elementary schools; eighteen from private schools. About twenty-five percent of the pupils enter the elementary school teaching profession; another twenty-five percent enter retail trade; ten percent take up engineering or other apprenticeships; ten percent go into manufactures; ten percent go into merchants' offices; eight percent become farmers; six percent become articled clerks or enter banks; and a very small percentage, about five percent, proceed to technical schools or other places of higher education.

There is no continuous teaching of vocal music in the school. This side of the curriculum should be strongly encouraged. The school rents cricket and football grounds from the local Cricket and Football Club, at a rent of £5 a year. It has the use of the ground in the day time, except on alternate Saturday afternoons.

The offices for both boys and girls are distinctly bad, and require immediate attention. The boys' cloak room is a mere lobby, without hot-water pipes. The girls' cloak room is used also as a cookery room and occasionally as a dining room. An assembly hall can be made by the joint use of the two larger rooms. The whole school, however, is not assembled together every day. This is a weak spot in the organisation of the school.

Heanor is a good collecting ground for pupil teachers. More boys from this district become pupil teachers than is usually the case in the neighbourhood. This fact is largely owing to the personal influence of the rector, Mr Corfield.

Recommendations

The future of this school will be much affected by the opening of an attractive higher grade school in Ilkeston. In time past, Heanor has drawn pupils from places which would more naturally be served from elsewhere. The circumstances of Heanor would make it inexpedient to establish a truly secondary school here. There are very few middle-class people in the neighbourhood. The industries of the district are mining, a little iron-working, engineering and the manufacture of hosiery.

The action of the Science and Art Department in developing its organised science schools, and then subsequently calling them secondary schools, has resulted in what is practically a misnomer in the case of Heanor. Heanor is in effect a higher grade elementary school, and I would recommend the Committee to recognise it on this basis in future.

No one can predict with certainty the numbers of children who will wish to go to the Heanor School when the other schools have been opened in Ilkeston and Long Eaton. The present school should be thoroughly re-decorated and cleaned, and the offices and cloak room accommodation much improved.

Heanor is a suitable place for a pupil teacher centre. The present pupil teacher centre should be re-organised and made a day centre in connection with the Heanor Secondary and Technical School, or, as I would suggest its being called in future, 'The Heanor Higher Grade Elementary School.'

The whole responsibility for giving the instruction at the pupil teacher centre should, of course, rest with the staff of the centre. The head teachers of the public elementary schools where the pupil teachers would go for their experience would give professional instruction in the art of teaching. Great care should be taken not to overwork the pupil teachers during the time they are serving in the elementary schools.

Fortunately, the suggestion that the name of the school be changed to the 'Heanor Higher Grade Elementary School' was not followed (though we only have a few years to wait before the next name change!) Sadler's suggestions regarding the establishment of a pupil teacher centre, however, were progressed and developed over the next few years.

At this time, the school was split into five classes. There were 23 juniors, with an average age of 12 years. The 1st year elementary course had 59 pupils with an average age of 12.8 years. The 2nd year elementary course had 33, average age 13.8 years. After this, numbers dropped, with 13 pupils taking the 1st year advanced course (average age 14.5 years). The 2nd year advanced course, designed for a small class of students preparing for the intermediate county scholarship examination, had just six pupils, also aged 14.5 years on average.

The curriculum included, for all classes, religious knowledge, English, history and geography, French, mathematics, natural science and drawing. All classes except the 2nd year advanced course also had drill and shorthand on their timetable. Natural science meant, for the juniors, physics together with some botany and natural history; for the rest, it was physics and chemistry. Geometry appeared as a separate subject in the second and third years. Latin was taught as a 'crash course' in the 1st year advanced course only, to a small select group. In the second and third years, boys took woodwork and girls cookery and needlework.

Total class-teaching hours were 27½ per week and homework ranged from ½ hour per night for the juniors to 1½ hours per night for the 2nd year advanced pupils.

The emphasis on science and technical subjects in the curriculum at this time comes through clearly. Taking the 2nd year elementary course, after which the majority of pupils left school, as an example, 6 hours were devoted to physics and chemistry, 6½ hours to mathematics and geometry, 3½ hours to drawing; two hours to craft; and one hour to shorthand. So 19 hours, or two-thirds, of pupils' study time were devoted to these subjects. This left only two hours for English, two hours for history and geography combined, three hours for French, one hour for religious knowledge; and a half-hour for drill. The title 'Technical School' was no misnomer!

As an unusual aside, Ralph Stoddard appears to have been able to turn his hand to anything scientific. A newspaper report in September 1905 quoted a local resident bemoaning that persons injured in accidents in the area were having to make the trip to Nottingham in order to receive an X-ray, when the School had a perfectly good X-ray machine, and somebody (the Headmaster) who knew how to operate it!

Sadler's statistics reported on the careers of pupils leaving the School, showing that their education meant that few, if any, of the boys went into mining, as most of their contemporaries in the area must have done. Rather, as with the girls, they were more likely to take up white-collar occupations, or move into the professions. A teaching career was especially likely, and a small, but ever-increasing number, moved on to university after school. Since only a relatively small proportion of pupils came from middle-class homes, these statistics indicate that the School rapidly became an instrument for social mobility; and it can be assumed that this function was very much in the mind of its founders.

By the time of the HMI inspection in 1907, the number of pupils had risen to 331 – this in a school which was crowded with 134! The School now had 30 pupil teachers, and this class was initially based in the Wesleyan Centenary Hall, on Market Street (where Somerfield Supermarket now stands). Pupils were using every single inch of the school premises, and some were in the Church Institute on Ilkeston Road. The assistant staff had increased to eight masters and seven mistresses.

Although the HMI report itself is lost, Mr Stoddard quoted a few isolated comments from it in his 1949 Review.

> *The floor of the Manual Room threatens to collapse...*
>
> *The most satisfactory part of the accommodation is the Chemical Laboratory...*
>
> *The spirit and energy with which the whole staff works merits nothing but praise...*
>
> *The teaching hours of the whole staff are long and arduous...*
>
> *Despite the great difficulties, the standard of work seems to have been well maintained and that excellent result can only have been secured by the unremitting care on the part of the Headmaster and the most loyal co-operation of his staff...*

Music – accommodation very inadequate. There is no Hall or Assembly Room. There is no School pianoforte, the only one in the building was lent by the Headmaster about ten years ago. It is now quite worn out. The teacher in charge of the Violin Class is very enthusiastic and hopes for an Orchestra soon....

The chemical laboratory mentioned was in fact in a separate outbuilding which continued in use after the new School was built, as a workshop of the Heanor UDC, until it was demolished to make way for the new science block in 1959. The teacher of the violin class was Mr Enoch Shaw, who had some thirty pupils. It is interesting that the tradition of successful music making, which continued until the end of the School in 1976, began so early. The musical talents of the pupils were also demonstrated vocally; throughout the early years of the century, frequent references to concerts performed by the Heanor Technical Glee Choir can be found in the local press, sometimes accompanied by dramatic performances by pupils.

Heanor Secondary School staff, around 1909.
Rear: Mr Doran, Mr Howse, Mr Parsons.
Centre: Mr Barnes, Miss Manock, Miss Sheldon, Miss Mitchell, ?
Front: Mr Clarke, Miss Howe, Mr Stoddard, Miss Baguley, Mr White.

Press coverage of school sports revealed a move which, in today's society, may appear a little unusual. At the 1905 sports day, the first event mentioned was the 'shooting competition'. Shooting was strongly encouraged by the government and the School found a suitable site and acquired rifles and ammunition. With his military background, Mr W. Rodway Barnes led the group, along with two other teachers, Mr J.A. Doran and Mr S.E. Howse. The School team was well regarded, and in 1908 sent a team to the National Rifle Association competition at Bisley; the team, which included the Headmaster's son Ralph Cyril Stoddard, won bronze medals.

Of course, shooting was not the only sport at the School. Mr Stoddard recalled the years 1908 and 1909 as having the finest football team ever, with three of the pupils going on to play league football. Hockey was the favourite team sport for the girls. The issue, for both sports, was that the School did not own a sports ground. In 1908, Mr Stoddard took out a lease on the recreation ground (off Wilmot Street) from Mr Mundy, and he spent £400 of his own money in improvements. Subsequently, the Heanor UDC required this land for a public recreation ground, and the Headmaster was reimbursed.

Chapter 4

The New School

One thing was certain - a substantial increase in accommodation had to be found quickly!

A number of problems stood in the way of physically extending the size of the school, but perhaps the most serious of these was the fact that the School was in rented property. Furthermore, the 14-year lease was rapidly coming to an end. As early as 1895 discussions had taken place regarding the possibility of an outright purchase of the site from the Mundy estate. This however came to nothing. It was again discussed when the new County Education Committee was established, but the County did not want to do anything until they had received Sadler's report.

We have already seen that the School was finding additional space by using other accommodation in the town. As a stopgap measure, in December 1905 the C.E.C. recommended that a temporary wooden and iron building be erected next to the School to accommodate pupil teachers. This was later described by H.L. Harlow as '... *a small wooden building ... divided into two rooms with a partition so flimsy that it was easily possible for two concurrent lessons to become unbearably, though sometimes comically, confused.*'

At the start of 1906, the Heanor Urban District Council purchased Heanor Hall and its site from Mr A.E.M. Mundy, with the approval of the C.E.C. The District Council raised a loan of £4,100 for the purchase of the site '*with a view to the erection of additional buildings for the Secondary School and Pupil Teacher Centre*'. Interestingly, although the main purpose of the purchase was for education, the council yearbook shows that they also wished to use it for a '*Fire Station, and other purposes*'.

The new temporary building offered only a little respite to the growing pressure on space at the site. By the end of 1906, Heanor Education Committee was already asking that the county architect be instructed to examine the School with a view to providing additional accommodation. Furthermore, the Board of Education in London were becoming increasingly impatient about the inadequate facilities at Heanor, for they wrote to the County that they were not prepared to recognise the School for grant purposes beyond 1908 '*unless a satisfactory scheme for structural improvement is placed before the Board'*. Improvements were being planned, but in the interim, the County wrote that *'the only solution of the temporary difficulty will be the provision of another iron building...'*

This next temporary building, which was erected in 1907/8, was to become known as the 'Tin Tab', due to its similarity to the buildings often put up at the time as chapels or churches. It was to last until 1975. The cost exceeded the amount originally set aside, as the site chosen required additional excavation and brickwork. Mr Stone recalls:

> *This final comment* [about the foundations] *will come as no surprise to those who knew the 'Tin Tab' in its final days in the early 1970s, for then the floor in one room gave way to reveal a deep cavity below into which at least one boy disappeared, or was dumped. Nevertheless, when the building was finally demolished as unsafe, much of the woodwork, apart from the floors, was still in good condition.*

With the major hurdle of ownership of the site resolved, there was still the issue, highlighted by Sadler, of Ilkeston and its intentions. With these two issues in mind, the County Education Committee set up a Sub-Committee to consider the needs of both Ilkeston and Heanor. This Sub-Committee reported in October 1907 and recommended:

1) a new building at Heanor for 250 (25 pupil teachers).
2) a new school at Ilkeston for 250 (25 pupil teachers).
3) both to be dual schools with separate playgrounds, and class instruction so far as possible for the two sexes.
4) fees for both to be £5 for county and £7/10s for out-of-county pupils.
5) in repaying capital expenditure, the area in which the schools were situated should pay at least a double share in proportion to the rateable value as compared with outside areas served.
6) sufficient minor scholarships to be provided to meet the Board of Education's demand for 25 per cent free places.

Despite the recommendations, and the fact that Heanor had been operating as a mixed school for 14 years already, the County Council's Finance and General Purposes Committee had other ideas. They invited representatives from both Heanor and Ilkeston to meet to discuss an alternative proposal of a school entirely for girls at Heanor and a boys' school at Ilkeston, under a joint board of management.

Deputations from the two towns strongly objected to the proposal, and so the original recommendations were approved. It was stressed, though, that provision must be made for separate entrances, cloakrooms and playgrounds for boys and girls respectively. Both Heanor and Ilkeston were to have new Secondary Schools built, each to accommodate 250 pupils, and with provision for a limited number of pupil teachers. By February 1909, sketch plans of the new buildings at Heanor had been approved by governors.

The Heanor UDC wanted to keep that part of the site which included the outbuildings of the old Hall for council purposes, and there was some negotiation, involving modification of the plans of the School before the boundaries were agreed. These outbuildings continued to be used by the Council until the County Council acquired them in 1958 as part of the expansion programme for the School.

At this time, in 1909, a new governing body was constituted by the County Education Committee, its composition based on the smaller (but still very wide) area from which pupils still came. It consisted of 11 members from the Heanor UDC (six appointed by the Council from among its own members; two on the recommendation of the Derbyshire Education Committee, two on the recommendation of the local managers of Council and voluntary schools, and one *'woman of experience in education'*). Alongside the Heanor governors, there was to be one each from the parishes of Alfreton, Ripley, Horsley Woodhouse, Denby, Smalley and Pinxton, and one additional woman appointed by the Derbyshire Education Committee.

The formation of the new governing body was probably also the time of the change of the name of the School from the Heanor Technical and Secondary School to Heanor Secondary School. Certainly the change took place no later than this, for April 1909 saw the first edition of the Heanor Secondary School Magazine. (There had been a previous publication, 'The Old Tag-Hillian', but it is not known if any copies of this have survived.) The magazine was managed by a group of past and present pupils, and, with some gaps and several name changes, it continued until the end of the School. (Indeed, it still continues today, but that story comes later.)

From a school history writer's perspective, 1909 and 1910 are very special years. The school magazine, although often full of articles which tell us little about the events in School itself, is nevertheless a mine of information. For example, it is from the pages of the magazine that we learn, in April 1910, that pupils had to wear school caps (black and amber), or straw hats with black and amber ribbon. In the same edition, readers discovered that the School had sent a donation to the British Antarctic Expedition led by Captain Scott; one of the dogs on the ill-fated trip had accordingly been given the name 'Heanor'. The July 1911 edition even told you where to buy the 'the School colours', namely Rowell's outfitters on the Market Place, a shop which only finally closed in 2007. The school magazine is the source of much of the information in this book.

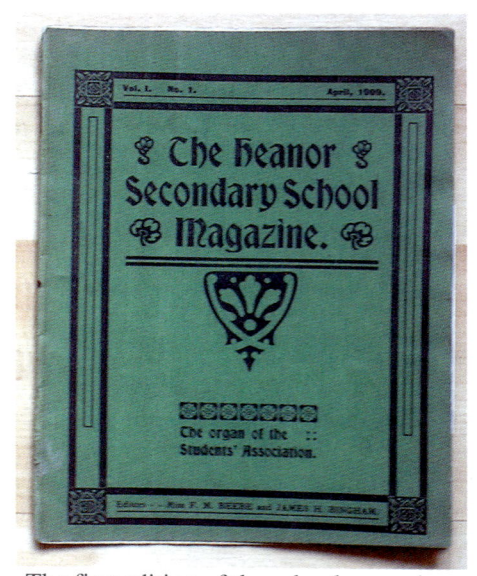

The first edition of the school magazine, April 1909.

The other principal source of information is that contained in the minute books of the school governors; the earliest minutes date from 25 October 1910, and are now kept at the County Records Office in Matlock. It is clear that there was at least one preceding volume, probably for 1902-10, but this has not survived.

November 1910 saw the governors taking over from Heanor UDC the liabilities and maintenance of the School, including the payment of salaries, *'on their handing over the balance in hand at that date'*. This balance subsequently proved to be £217/10/6d. The estimates for 1910/11 were quoted: they showed expenditure of £2,353, including salaries and wages (£1,855), rent (£138) and other expenses (£360); income was £2,050, comprising fees, including county minor scholarships (£800), government grants (£1,089) and a proportion of the penny rate (£150). By now, the staff included 11 full-time and three part-time teachers, together with Mrs R. Grassby as *'Superintendent of the Physical Culture Class'*.

The Articles of Government of the School stated that the Headmaster's salary should not be less than £300 (Mr Stoddard was already on £350 a year). They also state:

No pupil under the age of 8.

No pupil, other than a Pupil Teacher, shall remain after the age of 18, except with the Governor's permission, but only then to age 19 on recommendation of the Headmaster.

The School is open to all Day Pupils residing with parents, guardians, near relations, or in the house of any person approved by the Governors, other than a member of staff.

Fees – No fee or gratuity shall be received from or on behalf of any pupil in the School except in accordance with the Rules of Payment which shall be made by the Governors and approved by the Committee, and shall provide for the payment of such tuition fee at the rate of not more than £8 and not less than £4-10-0d. The regulation as to the minimum amount of tuition fee to be paid shall not apply until the opening of the new school buildings.

Tenders for the new buildings were invited in the early months of 1910, and in May the tender of Evans Brothers was accepted in the sum of £14,306/7/3d, subject to various reductions bringing down the cost from £57/4/6d per head to £52 per head. In addition to the main building costs, a tender from Jerram and Co of £546/10s was accepted *'for the installation of heating apparatus'*, and that of G R Turner Ltd of Langley Mill of £90 *'for providing iron roof-trusses'*.

One of the first entries in the governors' minutes records that *'the Education Committee to save money had deleted the wainscoting from the specification of the new building. It was unanimously resolved to protest* [that they should] *not spoil the school for so small a saving on the cost'*. The Education Committee relented and agreed to the panelling at a cost of £400.

Mr Stone noted (in the 1970s):

> *This last decision was a wise one, for the panelling gave the interior of the building a feel and an appearance which distinguish it to this day. It has withstood the passage of almost 70 years and of many generations of pupils with little, if any, deterioration and has needed relatively little maintenance. At one time in the 1950s it was misguidedly painted but was fortunately restored to its natural shade in the 1960s.*

(The 1960s restoration was to a natural, dark oak, shade. Since the School's closure, it has been discovered that the original shade was light oak, and it has since been further restored to this original colouring.)

The minutes occasionally listed quite specific and detailed deliberations into minutiae relating to the new building. The Board of Education was insisting on two emergency staircases to be provided in the case of fire, but it was decided to omit these staircases and provide rope ladders instead! It was then reported that the architect '*had agreed with the Board of Education to provide emergency step ladders from the* [upper] *corridors to the Central Hall*'. These ladders were never provided, as the Board of Education dropped the requirement; but when the buildings were modernised in the early 1960s, two external fire escapes were fitted.

The biggest complication was that the new building was replacing a school which was still functioning, and which could not be demolished until its replacement was usable. This accounts for some of the unusual room designs at the rear of the building, for the new build was made to dovetail close to the structure of Heanor Hall, as a recent reconstructed map of the site demonstrates.

The plans for the hall, which were published as a fold-out supplement in the school magazine for December 1909, underwent several changes before the building was completed. A manual instruction room, which was planned for the Ilkeston Road side of the building, in mirror-image to the cookery room on the Wilmot Street edge, never materialised. (Indeed, the cookery room was not built initially either.) Another example was the physics laboratory, on the first floor over the Headmaster's study. This was planned as a small room with a small library next to it, but the Headmaster wanted it to be the same size as the chemistry lab, and stated that he would find somewhere else for the books!

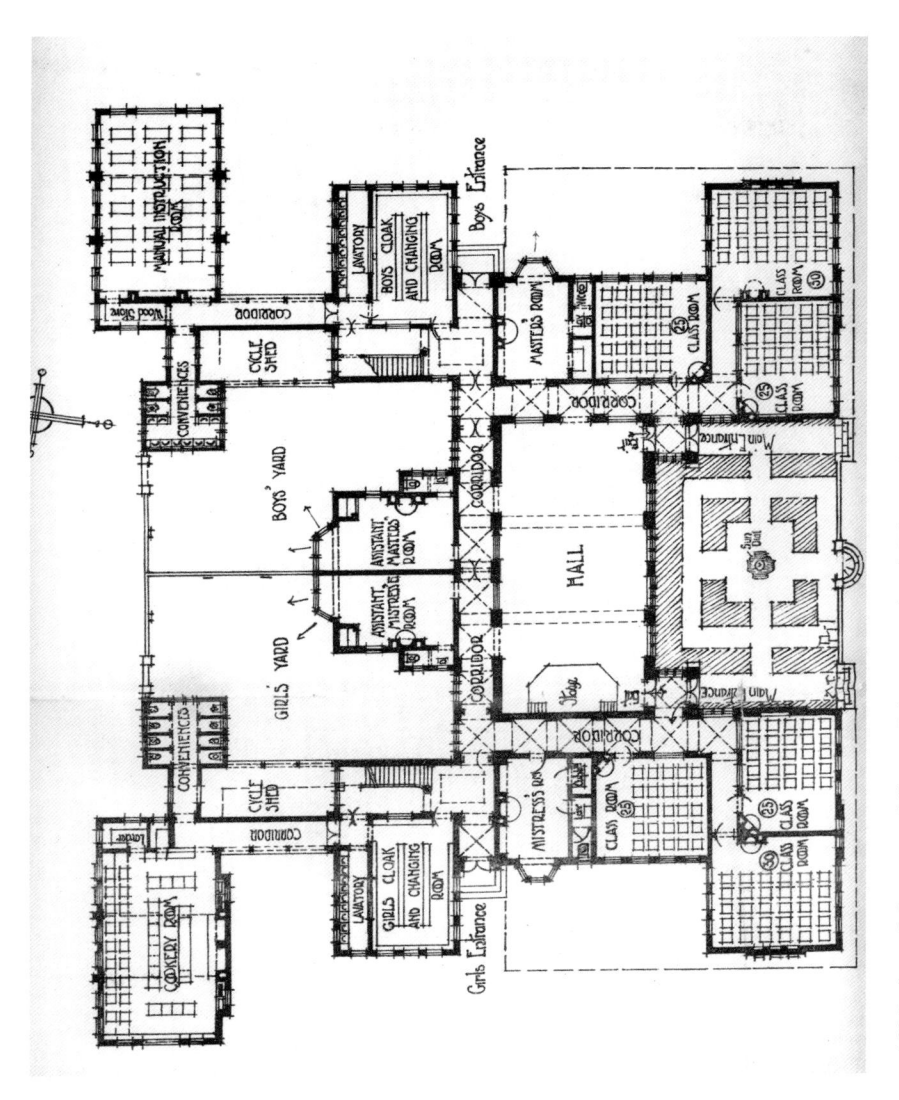

1909 plan of the ground floor of the new school. The cookery room and the manual instruction room were not built initially (the latter was never built).

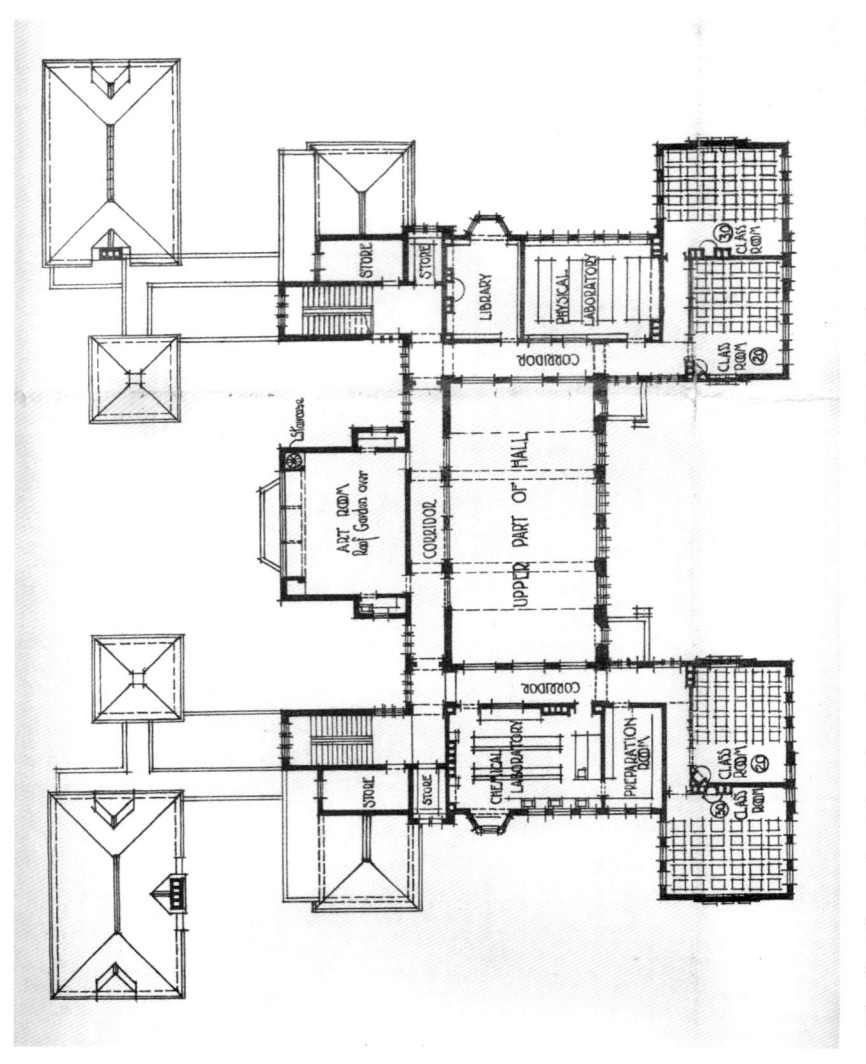

The first floor plan taken from the same school magazine. Note the planned library next to the physics laboratory.

Subsequently, the county architect agreed that suitable cupboards in each classroom be provided instead of a library. These cupboards were those with sliding doors to be found under the windows on the corridor of each classroom. It is interesting that by the end of its time as a school, the old physics laboratory was divided to provide the two rooms envisaged in the original plans.

The county architect wrote to the governors to say that *'it was customary for a stone-laying ceremony to be performed whenever a new secondary School was about to be erected'*. Such a ceremony was held on 12 November 1910, to which were invited past and present governors, members of the Heanor UDC, the chairman of each UDC or parish council in the school area, and local employers. The foundation stone is on the wall on the corner of the building nearest to the Mundy Street gate and was inscribed *'This stone was laid by John P Andrews, Esq, CC, Saturday November 12th 1910'*.

Photograph of the laying of the foundation stone, taken from a contemporary school magazine.

By the middle of 1911, the building work was clearly well advanced, for the governors recommended then that:

> ... *the whole of the front of the School be laid out as ornamental gardens, also that the whole of the trees remain excepting the yew tree near the main entrance... also that the wall in front of the ground at the corner of Wilmot Street and Mundy Street be lowered and iron railings fixed thereon... and that a portion of the ground at the corner of Wilmot Street and Mundy Street be given to the UDC to make the corner less dangerous.*

By July, it was reported to the governors that '*the contractor... would shortly commence to pull down the old premises*'. Throughout all this work, of course, the School continued in Heanor Hall. An editorial in the December edition of the school magazine stated that, '*The old school, as a building, is no more; but it is hoped that the spirit of the place, as embodied in the Old Students' Association, will still live on and flourish*'.

The April 1912 edition of the School Magazine reported:

> *The New School is now fast approaching completion. Occupation of the various rooms began in September last, and has gradually extended to the whole of one wing of the premises. The noise of the hammer has made the work of the Staff and the Pupils a matter of considerable difficulty.*

In the same edition, it was requested that pupils keep a spare pair of boots at school, so that they could get changed when arriving for the day.

Meanwhile, it was proposed that '*four stained glass windows be provided in the Central Hall*', with past and present scholars raising half the cost of £42. When the Education Committee refused to contribute the other half of the cost, it was then proposed to put one window in each staircase. Eventually, two windows were installed in the hall, and are still there. Each window shows a semi-biblical figure, one representing Science, the other Literature; the former carries a skull in one hand and a lantern in the other, the latter a quill and a book. The school magazine told readers that the windows were installed in the name of the Old Students, '*as a memento of the old school, together with tablets to the memory of the late Mr Thomas Mayfield and the late secretary Mr H. Grassby*'. Mr Mayfield had been the chairman of the committee which originally established the Technical School back in 1893, and subsequently became chairman of the governors; the manager of Morley's factory, he died in 1910. The plaque is no longer in situ, and has not been for many years, its whereabouts now unknown. As early as 1930, the plaque had fallen off; the governors agreed that it should be re-fixed, but there is no record as to whether this was actually done.

In April 1912, the governors were already aware of deficiencies in the new building, for they resolved that '*the question of providing a dining room for the scholars be considered at the next meeting*', and that '*the provision of a playground and rifle range be left to local members...*'.

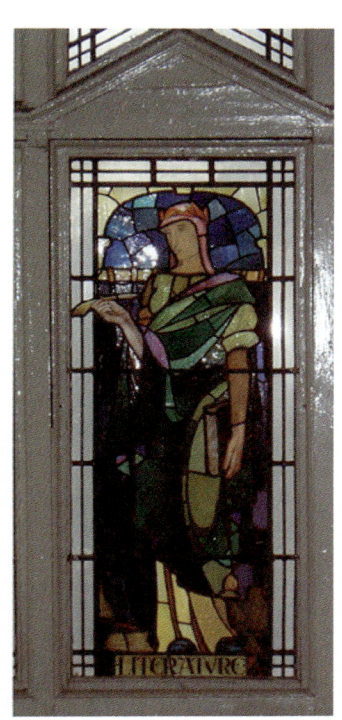

Modern photographs of the 1912 stained glass windows – Science and Literature.

During the period of the building work, the Education Committee took out a lease from the District Council on the site of the hall together with '*a portion of the garden and buildings thereto belonging*', approximately 5,868 sq. yards. The term of the lease was to be sixty years, with power to determine at the end of thirty years. The rent was to be, for the first 17 years £138/9s per annum, for the next 39 years £62/13s and for the remaining period five shillings per annum. The County Council covenanted to build on the land a secondary school costing £10,000 at least, to complete it by March 1913 and then to insure it.

At their meeting on 16 July 1912 they agreed on the arrangements for the formal opening of the new building. The School was opened at a ceremony on 11 September 1912, by Mr H. FitzHerbert Wright, MP. He was supported at the ceremony by Colonel J.E.B. Seeley, Secretary of State for War, and MP for the Ilkeston constituency, and Alderman James Oakes, JP, High Sheriff of

Derbyshire. The church was represented by the current member of the Corfield dynasty, Rev. Ashley T. Corfield. Mr Wright was presented with a golden key at the opening ceremony.

Putting the finishing touches to the school hall – October 1912.

The December magazine gave a full description of the School, with its '*ten classrooms, providing accommodation for 250 pupils*'. The article includes information that:

> *Two tennis courts have been provided and space has been left for the erection of a cookery room, and also for a dining room. Owing to the large number of students who stay for the midday meal, it is probable that these rooms will have to be erected sooner than was expected.*

So Heanor Secondary School now had a new building, and Heanor Hall had ceased to exist. There were those who mourned the passing of the grand old house, hoping that Heanor would again be chosen by a 'gentleman' for his place of abode. But, for the generations of pupils in education then, and to follow, the new school would provide excellent facilities. No major changes were required for many years, and even the name would be left untouched for over 30 years!

Chapter 5

War and Politics 1910 - 1919

The autumn term, 1912, began with the new school, full of all mod cons, and a great deal of enthusiasm, rightly justified.

In that academic year, the School published a new prospectus, in booklet format, complete with photographs of the exciting new classrooms (or rather the science laboratories and craft workshop).

The chemistry laboratory, in the 1912 prospectus.

The booklet began by listing the staff, Mr Stoddard and eight assistant masters and six assistant mistresses. It went on to name the board of governors, now chaired by John Andrews JP, a well known name in the vicinity. A potted history of the school was then followed by general notices, which are now repeated here in full:

ADMISSION TO THE SCHOOL. September is the month in which pupils should enter the School. An entrance examination is held by the Head-Master at the commencement of the Session in September of each year. Pupils (except Juniors) cannot as a rule be admitted during the months of January to July unless specially qualified.

Parents or Guardians (excepting Juniors) admitted to the School, must sign an agreement to pay the Governors £2, should the said pupil be withdrawn from School before the expiration of 3 years, except in case of serious illness, removal from the district, or other satisfactory reason.

Parents are particularly requested not to enter pupils who have no likelihood of attending for the minimum period of 3 years.

CURRICULUM. The Curriculum is designed for pupils who enter the School before, or immediately they are 12 years old. Candidates will generally be refused admission who are 13 years old and upwards.

The centre of the educational system in the School is a general course occupying the four years of the pupil's career from the age of 12 to the age of 16. This period is the main epoch of a pupil's education in a Secondary School.

To prepare for this 4 years' course, pupils over 8 years of age are admitted to the Junior School and are taught by a competent Junior Mistress.

THE SCHOOL COURSE. English, Mathematics, and Practical Science occupy a very prominent position in the work of the School as a whole. Cooking and Sewing are important subjects in the domestic training of the girls.

The subjects of the curriculum are:- Scripture, English, Geography, History, Mathematics, Chemistry, Physics, Botany, French, Art, Woodwork, Sewing, Cookery, Hygiene, Singing, Physical Exercises.

Special arrangements are made for tuition in Latin to pupils over 13 years of age, after consultation with the Head-Master.

Time is set aside in School hours for organized games, and all children who are physically fit are expected to take part. A 25 yards Rifle Range is provided in charge of a competent instructor.

A Library is provided for each form in the School, under the control of the Form teacher, and pupils may borrow books therefrom.

HOME LESSONS should not occupy more than 1 hour each evening in Forms III and IV, or 2 hours in the highest Forms. It is requested that the Head-Master be informed of cases in which a much longer or shorter time is taken. Homework during June and July is optional.

REGULAR AND PUNCTUAL ATTENDANCE *is expected from all. In every case of absence a written statement from parent or guardian must be brought on resumption of attendance by the pupil, who must then see the Head-Master. A Medical Certificate is necessary after illness.*

<u>A HIGH STANDARD OF CONDUCT</u> *is expected of all pupils who, so long as they remain members of the School, are answerable to the Head-Master for their conduct both in School and in public from the time they leave home.*
The Head-Master may suspend from further attendance at School any pupil who in his opinion is exercising a bad influence, bringing discredit on the School, or failing to profit by its advantages.

DRESS. Every boy must wear the School cap, or a straw hat with the School ribbon. Every girl must wear a straw sailor hat with the School ribbon. Girls are expected to wear the School Gymnasium Dress and suitable shoes at Physical Exercises.

THE TUITION FEE, which includes the cost of Books, Stationery, and all tuition is £1 10s 0d per Term to pupils under 12 years of age, and £2 0s 0d per Term to pupils over 12. The Text Books remain the property of the School.
The Fee must be paid during the first week of each Term.

HOURS OF ATTENDANCE. The hours of attendance are from 9.15am to 12.20, and 1.40 to 4pm. There is no School on Saturdays. The Head-Master will be pleased to see parents by appointment.

EXAMINATIONS. General School Examinations are held usually at the end of each Term by the Head-Master. Pupils are prepared for the Senior Local Examinations, the London University Matriculation, and Open Scholarships.

A REPORT of each pupil's attendance, conduct, and progress is sent to the Parent or Guardian at Xmas and Midsummer.

A SCHOOL MAGAZINE is issued terminally, containing matters of interest to both past and present pupils of the School, all of whom are invited to contribute articles for insertion therein.

The welfare of the girls has been specially considered, and a room is set apart, during the daytime, for their convenience under the supervision of the Senior Mistress.

The Senior Mistress is responsible under the Head-Master for the conduct of the girls; all questions concerning their conduct are referred to her and where necessary she will arrange interviews with parents.

Damage to School furniture must be immediately reported to the Form teacher. Pupils are expected to co-operate in the duty of upholding the dignity and cleanliness of the whole Institution.

The class rooms are to be entirely vacated and ventilated at 11am, and at the mid-day interval 12.20 to 1.40pm.

Pupils who are late for School must sign their names in the Late Book.

A Record Book is kept in each form of pupils whose conduct is not satisfactory. Such pupils must see the Head Master each Thursday, at 3pm.

ENTRANCE SCHOLARSHIPS:-
I.   Scholarships to the value of Fees, Railway Fares, and Books awarded annually, tenable for 3 years, are
(a)   Minor Scholarships.
(b)   Richardson Scholarships
(c)   Langley Mill Co-operative Scholarships.
II.   Scargill Scholarships, of the value of £10 to £15 approximately, awarded to pupils residing in West Hallam and neighbourhood.
III.   Turner Scholarships, of the value of £10, awarded to pupils residing in Alfreton and neighbourhood.

SCHOLARSHIPS AWARDED TO PUPILS IN THE SCHOOL:-
I.   Scholarships to the value of Fees and Books, awarded by the Governors of the School to Fee-paying pupils who have completed a 3 years' course, as per agreement, and have reached Form VI.
II.   Intermediate and Major Scholarships, awarded by the County Education Authority.

Many of the rules listed would still apply to schools today, but others are interesting if only for being anachronistic. Of particular note is the 'fine' for taking pupils out of school before they had completed the full three years. (This was to be raised from £2 to £3, and the period committed to was raised from three years to four years, in 1919.) A recurring theme in the governors' minutes was the receipt of letters from parents asking to be excused this payment. The normal reason for this was that the pupil was taken out of school as soon as he or she had reached the minimum school leaving age, in order to start work. It is of note, at a time when the school leaving age was 12 years, that the School expected pupils to stay until they were 16 – clearly the aim of the School was to push its scholars on to higher things. Also of interest was the minimum age in the junior class – this was very shortly (July 1914) to be raised from eight to ten. Whilst some pupils attended from this age, the other local schools provided training to equip their more gifted pupils to take the scholarship exams at the age of 12. There was no reference to the forms of punishment used at the school, but there can be little doubt that a visit to the Headmaster's office on a Thursday afternoon would not have been a pleasant experience!

The prospectus ended with an 'Honours List' of successes achieved by previous students, including several who had since gone on to obtain university degrees. Considering the report from Sadler regarding the nature of the population, this was no mean achievement, and the School was quite rightly proud of itself.

The new School in 1913.
The lady in the photograph is Mary Sharratt, wife of the photographer.

Perhaps because the School was newly built and equipped, or perhaps just because it was time, the beginning of 1913 saw another visit from H.M.

Inspectors. It is likely, with everything looking so rosy from the outside, that everyone expected a glowing report.

As previously mentioned, we do not know what the report actually said, as it does not survive, though we do, through the uproar it caused, have some of the report's summary. The report caused an absolute furore, the aftermath of which was still in progress the following year, and almost ripped apart the School's staff and governing body.

Minutes of meetings are often frustrating, in that they do not record the whole picture, as the participants are already aware of some facts which we, nearly a hundred years later, do not know. This case is no exception.

At the governors' meeting on 8 May 1913, a single extract from the HMI report was minuted, namely that, '*it cannot be said that the staff appears to be a particularly united body*'. That is all, but the governors would, undoubtedly, have read the entire report. The governors immediate reaction was to dismiss two of the assistant masters, Mr J.A. Doran and Mr E.A. Parkinson. It was also resolved that the chairman should speak to a third member of staff, Mr W.R. Barnes, with regard to his conduct. Subsequent reports clarify that the HMI report itself did not name any individual members of staff, though no doubt the inspectors would have discussed their findings with the governors.

At the following meeting, on 10 June 1913, it was revealed that Mr Stoddard had been given leave of absence due to illness until the start of the autumn term – this on full pay. Mr Clarke was to be the Acting Headmaster in the interim. At this meeting, Mr Doran and Mr Parkinson were asked to leave the school in July. A few days later, a replacement was chosen for Mr Doran, and the following month for Mr Parkinson. (Mr Parkinson resigned rather than having to be dismissed.)

It was not, however, going to be quite that simple for the School to deal with the criticism, for Mr Doran had by now engaged Robinsons solicitors to act on his behalf. A letter was received from them, demanding to see a copy of the inspection report. This was referred to the Department of Education, and subsequently refused, on the grounds that the report was confidential.

Articles in the local newspapers show that there was much more activity taking place than just the discussions at the governors' meetings. Mr Doran had taken his case to the Heanor Trades Council, and spoke at a public meeting of the Marlpool and Langley Ratepayers Association. Mr Doran protested that he had never had an adverse report during his ten years at the school, and the Association agreed to call a public protest meeting on his behalf. It was also discussed at the Urban District Council Meeting (bear in mind that all the key governors were also councillors). At the council meeting, Mr Andrews, chairman of the governors, stated, '*Mr Doran was one of those whom the Governors thought it would be an advantage to the School if he were asked to resign*'. Mr Andrews went on to state that if the Council believed that he had taken the wrong course of action, then he would resign. Councillor Bassford was unhappy that the subject had been raised at the UDC meeting, but at the end of the proceedings the Council passed a vote of confidence in the governors.

Councillor H. Bassford was in quite a difficult position. He was a member of the governors of the School, but he was also chairman of the Trades Council which had taken up Mr Doran's cause. At the August meeting of the UDC, Mr Bassford asked that the Council be given a copy of the HMI report, but this was turned down. Meanwhile, the Trades Council wrote to the governors wanting to know why, if Mr Doran was being charged with causing '*a mutiny among the staff*', Mr Stoddard had not done something about it earlier. Mr Doran had further cause to complain, when, at the start of the new term, he was not allowed to teach at evening classes in the town either. The first governors' meeting of the new academic year saw the Rev. Ashley Corfield team up with Councillor Bassford in seeking the publication of the previous HMI report, after Mr Andrews stated that the inspectors had complained for years about the '*tone of the school*'.

At a public meeting in October Mr Bassford, who was in possession of the full report, stated that it was his opinion that Mr Doran and Mr Parkinson had been made scapegoats. He offered to make the report public if sufficient rate-payers asked him to do so. A petition was set up, and over 500 names were added. As a result, a public meeting was held under the auspices of the Trades Council at the end of November in the Town Hall, and Mr Bassford read out the entire report. The Ripley and Heanor News said that the report, which took an hour to read, was '*voluminous, largely technical, and somewhat difficult to follow*'. However, it printed the concluding summary of the report in full:

> *It would be the merest affectation to pretend that all is well with the School at the present time. On the purely intellectual side there is some*

good, indeed, excellent individual teaching, but much of the effect even of this is spoiled by want of co-operation. There is a general slackness and want of organisation and discipline, which cannot fail to prevent the school from doing all that it might and should be doing. The Headmaster must get to know more about his school; the staff must cultivate a stronger corporate feeling amongst themselves; the pupils must learn to obey rules with more readiness; and all must work more loyally together for the good of the school. Not until this is done and the whole organisation receives the 'tightening up' of which it is badly in need, will the school be in a position either to do the best work of which it is, or should be capable, or become that centre of light and leading to Heanor and surrounding district which a good secondary school ought properly to be.

Specific criticisms of the school by the inspectors were itemised in the news report.

> The Headmaster needed to find a way of reducing the work done for the four evening schools he ran.
>
> There was too fast a turnover of female staff.
>
> Teachers, even those teaching the same subject, did not appear to know what each other was teaching.
>
> The Headmaster could not remember when the last staff meeting was held.
>
> Likewise, the Headmaster could not give any clear indication as to what the role of the senior mistress was.
>
> A school prefect system had been introduced just a few days prior to the arrival of the inspectors.
>
> Discipline was poor, especially amongst the girls (the inspectors cited an incident at a railway station).
>
> Uniform rules were disregarded.
>
> There were no school societies.

Staff photograph, 1913.
Rear: Mr Clarke, ?, Mr Barnes, Miss Sheldon, ?, Mr Howse, Mr Fox.
Front: Miss Shortridge, Mr Parsons, Miss Watson, Mr Stoddard, Miss Baguley, Mr Cowell, Miss Manock, Mr White.

53

The view of the meeting was that Mr Doran, who was described as a very popular teacher, had been unfairly dismissed. There was also much criticism of Mr Stoddard: *'The Governors did not dismiss the man who did not organise, but sent him on a holiday at £1 a day, and the ratepayers paid for it'*.

The following month, the governors cast a vote of censure against Mr Bassford, but he appears to have been unrepentant. Mr Doran took the Derbyshire County Council to court. The minutes of the County's Finance and General Purposes Committee recorded that a County Court Summons had been served on them, claiming five months' salary (£64/11s/8d). The Council determined to fight the case and appointed a barrister. Whilst we do not know what the legal opinion was, we can perhaps hazard a guess when, just five weeks later, the Committee decided to settle the case out of court and offer Mr Doran £40 plus up to £10 costs. As a postscript, in June 1914, the Ripley and Heanor News announced: *'The many friends and former pupils of Mr J.A. Doran, formerly on the teaching staff of Heanor Technical School, will learn with pleasure that he has been appointed a master in a Roman Catholic school in the vicinity of Bath.'*

During all this turmoil, of course, school life, and day-to-day decision making, had to continue as normal, though there was some impact due to the absence of the Headmaster; the school magazine, for example, was not published in the Spring or Summer of 1913. By the start of the 1913/4 academic year, the School had 239 pupils, including 57 new starters – by the middle of the term, the number had reached 250, which was, of course, the designated enrolment for the School.

The reorganisation following the Education Committee's report of 1907, saw the catchment area of the Heanor Secondary School much reduced, and in 1914 the new Ilkeston County Secondary School opened. However, pupils still came from a very wide area, including Ilkeston. The Headmaster's report in 1917 showed the distribution of pupils' home addresses: Heanor 42, Langley Mill 13, Aldercar 2, Marlpool 3, Eastwood, 17, Horsley Woodhouse 5, Kimberley 3, Kilburn 3, Langley 4, Loscoe 3, Codnor 11, Ripley 24, Codnor Park 4, Riddings 11, Pinxton 6, Coxbench 1, Somercotes 8, Swanwick 8, Alfreton 6, Ilkeston 25, Smalley 7, Denby 5, and Stanley Common 3.

Developments at the School in relation to building and equipment continued too. From the start of the new building, it had been recognised that the dining facilities were totally inadequate. This was rectified when, in October 1915, a new block, comprising both dining room and a new cookery centre, was opened. The dining room had space for 150, though 220 comfortably attended its opening day. Mr Stoddard had plans to turn the old dining room into a gym - this never happened. In 1916, the basement was fitted out with mining equipment, an *'air gallery, fan and motor'* to assist with technical training. Of significant long-term impact, the lease on the premises from the Urban District to the County Council was extended in October 1914 from 60 years to 999 years; this meant that the County need not fear future development at the site. At the same time, the County purchased an extra 3,000 square yards, with the provision that a small part of this would be given up for road widening. When this was completed, by the widening of Ilkeston Road and Mundy Street in March 1916, the old pond of Heanor Hall, fondly remembered for its dragonflies, was filled in.

At the annual sports day in July 1913, for the first time, the School was divided into three 'houses' in order to compete. Students were placed into their house according to where they lived. The houses were called, not very imaginatively, Eastern (wearing a green badge), Western (purple) and Central (red). The same system was followed in 1914, but in 1915 the system was changed and the houses were named after three people of local historical significance, namely Howitt (after William and Mary), Ray (after the previous owners of Heanor Hall), and Flamstead (after the first Astronomer Royal, from Denby). The colours now were Howitt white, Ray red, and Flamstead blue. It is doubtless not a coincidence that combined they made a patriotic red, white and blue. According to a previously prepared, but unpublished, history of the School,

> *... all pupils living within a two mile radius of Heanor were Rays, those west of this line were Flamstead and those east Howitt. After two years, this system was found not to be working, and the houses were given an equal number of pupils.*

Whether playing for the house or for the School, pupils were offered a varied array of sports. By 1914, the boys were making regular trips to play against other football teams in Derbyshire and Nottinghamshire. That year also saw an attempt to introduce basketball for girls. The round-up of inter-house sports for the year included football, cricket, rounders, fencing, swimming, shooting and cross-country running. In the following year, there was mention of a swimming gala competition between the School and Langley Mill Boys' School, who won for the fourth consecutive year. Inter-house sports also included diving. (Langley Baths had been opened in 1902.) Skipping, with seven different competitions, was also subject of a separate inter-house tournament in 1915.

But sporting references began to take a back seat. The outbreak of the First World War in August 1914 was to become the biggest factor of the decade. Heanor and its schools were affected no less than any other community in the country.

The earliest reference in the governors' minutes was a decision, in October 1914, to allow the Committee for the Belgian Refugees to use school facilities free of charge. This was followed in June 1915 by a decision to exempt four Belgian refugees, who were pupils at the School by that time, from fees.

Like other schools around the country, staff and pupils were doing their bit for the war effort, and press and school magazine reports listed the Christmas parcels and knitting done by the girls for soldiers on the front. Fund-raising events were held, and Mr Stoddard reported that students were cultivating every possible spare piece of ground, some 1500 square yards, for growing vegetables.

The first report of an old student being killed in action was that of Harold Saxton, whose death was reported in December 1914. And gradually the number rose, until, by the end of the war, over 50 old boys had been killed. The reality of war came right to the heart of the school, when Flight Lieutenant Ralph Cyril Stoddard, of the Royal Flying Corps, the son of the Headmaster, was killed in action in July 1916. As early as 1916 discussion was taking place about the eventual raising of a memorial as a roll of honour. As soon as the war was over, the question of a memorial was referred to the Old Students' Association.

It was not, though, just the pain of losing old students. The school also had to deal with the complications of losing masters who were signing up. The biggest impact was undoubtedly the departure of Mr W.T. Clarke, the senior master, who signed up in February 1915 with the Royal Army Medical Corps (followed a few months later by another teacher, Mr Fox). At least two others, Mr Ostick and Mr Cowell, were also on active service by the end of the war.

These staff had to be replaced, at a time when all schools were suffering the same staffing shortages. The governors, as no doubt was taking place elsewhere, tried to find ways to prevent the situation worsening still further. When, in May 1918, a letter came to the School advising them that assistant teachers of military age could now be conscripted, they resolved to regrade one such assistant, Mr White, as a senior master. They also resolved that if he were called up, they would appeal, on the grounds that *'he is serving his Country better in his present occupation than he would in the army'*. Another assistant master, Mr Barnes, was to be advised to obtain a medical grading to prevent his call-up.

The war years did not see only bad news for individuals. The chairman of the governors, John Andrews, received the title Alderman in January 1917. In July 1918, the art master, William Rodway Barnes, exhibited a number of paintings at the Grafton Galleries in London, an exhibition which was visited by the King. And, in June 1918, Ralph Stoddard celebrated his 25th anniversary as Headmaster at the School. An evening event, organised by the Old Students' Association, saw presentations to both Mr Stoddard and his wife.

However, just before his anniversary, the problems which had beset Mr Stoddard returned. As with the earlier incident, we only get hints from reading the minutes of the governors' meetings, but things were still not happy in the School.

On 18 June 1918, Alderman Andrews read out his letter of resignation to the governors, which *'contained certain statements concerning Mr Stoddard'*, who was present at the meeting. The following week, the senior mistress, Miss Baguley, resigned, as did another mistress Miss Biss. (The post of senior mistress was now filled by promoting the French mistress, Miss Ellen Harrison Webb, who was to remain at the school until 1948.)

The governors at this stage set up a sub-committee to look into Alderman Andrews' resignation, which had not yet been accepted.

The July meeting was still chaired by Mr Andrews, and the principal business of the day was the report of the sub-committee. For a change, the minutes were quite thorough on that occasion, for reasons which would become apparent, and Mr Andrews' resignation letter was given in full. The letter was quite scathing in its criticism of the Headmaster, though it still left many questions unanswered, as a few quotes will show:

> … *I am fully convinced that a change of headship is not only desirable but it is a vital necessity in the interests of the School. Mr Stoddard has retained his position on so many occasions by a hair's breadth.*
>
> *Time after time we have evidence of mistrust from his staff…*
>
> *In January of this year, Mrs Stoddard stated to me that the school was full of treachery.*
>
> *I am convinced that his personal weakness is having a serious effect upon the efficiency of the school.*

Mr Andrews went on to state that staff had suspicions concerning '*the Oxford Exam Papers*', but no further explanation of this was given. Much of the letter was concerned with Mrs Stoddard, and her alleged interference at the School. One member of staff had accused her of '*being a thief*', but again this was not elaborated upon.

However, the main reason he gave for his resignation was that Mr Stoddard was duplicitous, praising people to their faces, and plotting behind their backs. He gave two specific examples of such behaviour. He also quoted an unnamed member of staff as having said, '*I would rather be kicked downstairs by a straightforward and honourable man, than I would be flattered by Mr Stoddard!*' As far as Mr Andrews was concerned, it was time for Mr Stoddard to go, but it appears that he was the only one of the governors to think this way, hence his resignation.

Mr Andrews went on to say,

> *I have been on fairly friendly terms with Mr Stoddard for many years. His bright conversational powers and in many respects his kind-heartedness, together with his great store of general knowledge have brightened many hours, but I am fully convinced that his personal weakness is having such a serious effect upon the efficiency of the school…*

Mr Andrews also blamed the recent resignation of the mistresses directly on Mr Stoddard.

The Sub-Committee, chaired by Rev. F.S. Boissier, the Denby representative on the governors, had sent a questionnaire to each member of staff. Six of the twelve teachers, who together had more than 50 years service had replied that they *'did not have unreserved confidence in the Headmaster'*. Those who did have confidence in him were considerably newer to the job, four of them being in their first year at the school. There were also concerns regarding his *'frankness'* in dealings with the staff.

The conclusion of the report made four recommendations, which were accepted by the governors. Three of them were relatively bland: they recognised the concern over staff mistrust in the Headmaster, they required the report and the chairman's letter to be fully minuted, and they asked the chairman to withdraw his resignation, which he did. The fourth, however, is interesting in that: *'Mrs Stoddard be told not to visit the school premises except on important business with Mr Stoddard, and at such time as the school is open to the public for entertainment or public function.'* In other words, the Headmaster's wife was banned from the school! However, there was no recommendation suggesting that any form of remedial action be taken against the Headmaster himself. Perhaps the governors considered that the mere fact that he had sat through all these discussions would be sufficient.

Ninety years later, what are we to make of this? Clearly, the staff were not totally happy working under Mr Stoddard's leadership. In view of the earlier issue regarding turnover of staff, this appears to have particularly affected the female teachers. There is also evidence that the Headmaster's wife took a more active role in school issues than was considered proper, and that this annoyed some staff, especially those whose job she was interfering with (such as the senior mistress). That said, no one ever expressed any concerns over Mr Stoddard as a teacher; in fact the contrary applies, as even Alderman Andrews found time to praise him while attacking him. Mr Stoddard was extremely well regarded in the area, and his single-handed establishment of the school 25 years previously is testimony to his abilities. Where he perhaps struggled was in his management of staff, something which had not been an issue when he first obtained the post. A former pupil, writing some 75 years after attending the School referred to Mr Stoddard as, *'a bit weak on discipline… the weaker teachers could not rely on him to back them up'*.

However, it must be borne in mind that we only have one version of events, and that Ralph Stoddard had no recorded right to reply. Alderman Andrews, a magistrate and local captain of industry, might have had his own views on how a school should be run. But it is clear that he did not have the full backing of his fellow governors, otherwise an alternative option, namely forcing Mr Stoddard to leave, could have been pursued.

The war finished in November 1918. The four masters mentioned earlier had all survived and would return. In December, Mr Clarke who had been mentioned in despatches, wrote to the governors asking them to break their own rules and accept his eight-year-old son as an 'unregistered' pupil – this they did, but not unanimously. He had returned to his old position at the School by the end of the winter, as had Mr Fox. The governors were now in a position where they had to work out what to do with the female staff who had been brought in to cover while the men were at war. A sub-committee was formed, and it was decided that Miss Beecroft would have to leave at the end of the term, and that Miss Hargreaves and Miss Chambers would be dismissed, in that order, upon the return of Mr Ostick and Mr Cowell. In those days before 'equal opportunities', the females certainly knew their place!

Mr Stoddard's final decade was not going to be as rough as 1913 – 1918, but at least one more major disagreement was to follow.

Chapter 6

Stoddard's Last Years – the 1920s

The new decade would see several notable departures, not least that of the Headmaster, as well as the arrival of new faces who would subsequently become well known in the area. It started with the retirement in March 1920 of the senior master, W.T. Clarke, who had been at the School since 1894. Mr A.J. White, who had already been at the School for 15 years, was promoted to senior master, and the vacancy was taken by Mr G.F. Hosegood. In June of the same year, Mr Cowell resigned, and was replaced by Joseph ('Joey') Hancock, who was to stay for 36 years. Due to increasing pupil numbers a request for additional staff was also submitted. One of the new staff was Miss Marjorie Dawson, who would stay at the school for 25 years. Another new starter who was destined to stay for the duration was geography master, H.G. Sears who started in 1921. Also just fitting into this chapter, leaving in the summer of 1929, was Mr S.E. Howse, who had been the woodwork teacher at the school for 22 years, and who had been involved in the School's early success at Bisley. Changes affected the governors too, for in May 1920, Alderman Andrews died. He was replaced temporarily by William Hardy, Mr H.B. Mayfield subsequently taking the post. Another change to the governors was the removal of representation of the Alfreton District in 1922 due to the opening of a secondary school at Swanwick.

The increasing paperwork of running a school also led to the first recruitment of a clerical assistant for the Headmaster in 1921.

As already mentioned, the question of an appropriate memorial to the fallen of the School had been passed to the Old Students' Association, and fund-raising was very much in evidence. Of course, this was not the only worthy cause in the town; for example, fund-raising for the Heanor Memorial Hospital was also continuing apace. Heanor Secondary School was one of only a few places in the area (the town hall and the Co-operative hall at Langley Mill being two others which spring to mind), where indoor fund-raising events, especially dances, could be held for relatively large numbers. The school hall was much in demand!

This caused quite a bit of discussion and conflict for the governors. They had to deal with a request (from a staff-member) that dancing be added to the curriculum – quickly refused as being '*not considered of sufficient importance*'. Harder to resolve, though, were objections from the local police, who pointed out, after a number of dances in support of the war memorial hospital fund, that the school needed a music and dancing licence. A visit to the superintendent by the governors to explain that they only held charitable events did not alter things. The County Education Office now insisted that no activity should take place which would require a licence, '*as exhibition of the necessary notice on the school building would be quite beneath the dignity of any school*'. In July 1923, the governors received a letter from the County noting that the School let its premises out far more often than other schools. Whilst leaving decision-making on this matter to the governors, they were reminded that '*as a rule lettings should only be for purposes which have some connection with the work of the school*'. The School kept turning requests down, so much so that the governors double-checked with County. Not only did the Education Office repeat that other schools did not find the need to rent their halls out as much, they also claimed that the woodwork at Heanor never seemed as well-cared for, a fact which they put down to all the dances. It was decided that they would let the hall out once a month, and only for purely charitable purposes. Later in the year, political meetings were added to the list of approved lettings.

Yet more problems arose for the Headmaster, but at least this was kept out of the newspapers. The governors' minutes for 19 December 1922, cryptic as always, reported briefly on an allegation made by the senior mistress, Miss Webb, regarding Mr Stoddard's conduct towards one of the pupils. No details were given but it was enough to appoint a sub-committee to investigate, and both Mr Stoddard and Miss Webb were interviewed. The sub-committee concluded that his actions had been misinterpreted, and that '*Mr Stoddard had no ulterior motive in as much as it took place in full view of the whole class of 25 girls*'. There was no information as to what the alleged incident involved. The Headmaster was exonerated. However, the fact that the senior mistress should feel the need to go to the governors with this, rather than deal with it directly with the Head, leads to the question whether all was yet well. Certainly this incident led to no lasting problems for the Headmaster.

In the first HMI inspection since 1913, which took place in 1924, the inspectors reported '*an efficient institution performing useful services which are appreciated in the neighbourhood. Much has been done to remedy certain grave defects which existed at the time of the last inspection'*. Indeed their report was generally favourable throughout.

The school magazine, which appears not to have been published since 1916, was relaunched in 1922. Now entitled 'The Magazine of the Heanor County Secondary School', the editor of the first editions was Herbert Vincent Youle, a former pupil recently appointed to the staff. The school magazine went to great lengths to cover the arrival and unveiling of the school war memorial and roll of honour, and the July 1923 edition included a photographic insert of the finished painting.

Centrepiece of the war memorial.
(The vertical line is from the glass cover which now protects the painting.)

The memorial took the form of a three-panel painting, which is sited in the old school hall to this day. The artist was Professor Caley Robinson, A.R.A., R.W.S., and the painting was exhibited at the Royal Academy prior to its arrival in Heanor. The central panel contains figures representing Faith,

The full Caley Robinson war memorial, 1923.

Justice, Charity, Fortitude and Hope, supported by heroes, martyrs and warrior saints. At the feet of the central figure of Charity are seated children of the present generation. At the base of this panel is the plaque containing the roll of honour, the names of the 57 old students who were killed in the Great War. The two side panels show British soldiers in the field of battle, and those who served their country at home.

The painting was unveiled at a ceremony on 19 June 1923, by an old student, Major H.J. Humphrys D.S.O., M.C. The dedication was carried out by Rev. S. Gething Caulton, and addresses were given by Mr Stoddard and Mr Mayfield, as well as Major Humphrys. A number of songs and hymns were sung (but not *To be a Pilgrim*). At the end of the event, hundreds of members of the public filed through the hall to view the memorial.

Throughout the early twenties, the School, like the rest of society, was moving into a new age of technology. The first request from the governors for a telephone to be installed was in June 1920 (though there had been an exchange at Langley Mill since the turn of the century). The following year the first of several requests was submitted for electric lighting. A new typewriter was purchased in 1921 (though they had one previously), and the School obtained a duplicator in 1922. The year after that was especially exciting, as a wireless was bought, at an amazing cost of £70, followed the month afterwards by a new piano (which cost £60, and was only to be used for school purposes – not for dancing!) And in 1924, the School purchased a gramophone, for the purpose of *'teaching correct pronunciation of the French language'*.

As we have already seen, sports facilities had been a difficulty from the beginning of the School in 1893. The improvements offered by the new School included two new tennis courts, but they were still having to rely on renting fields from the District Council for other sports. The school magazines of the 1920s showed that sports activities were popular, with reports of the School's football, cricket and hockey teams, plus tennis, and, of course, the annual sports day. The District Council now owned the recreation ground on Wilmot Street, which the School had previously leased for its exclusive use, but this was still being rented on a weekly basis. It is clear from the governors' minutes that, by this time, the School was also using another field, called Burrows Field, also rented from the UDC, but they had nothing they could call their own. Approaches were made to the Council, asking for eight acres of a site off Ilkeston Road, which they had recently acquired for housing purposes.

The Council turned the request down, but did offer the School (for rental) the *'field occupied by the Sye Lane Institute Football Club'*. A sub-committee was set up in 1921 to look into this issue.

Throughout this period, letters were passing to and fro between the School and the County Education Office. The Education Office must have felt somewhat pestered by all this, along with the regular requests for electricity – no doubt every other school in the county was making similar demands. In June 1924, they asked the governors to make their minds up: which was most important, electric lighting or a school playing field? Diplomatically, the School replied that they hoped the County could provide both, but their request for electricity could wait until they had a definitive answer on a playing field.

The Heanor UDC had been asked in December 1923 if they would sell, rather than rent, seven or eight acres of land to the School. Negotiations continued throughout 1924, and the County Education Committee finally decided that they would support the purchase of a playing field, also stating, *'If large enough, it might possibly provide a site for the contemplated technical school.'* This, of course, is what eventually happened, and it will be touched on again in the next chapter. It was not until the summer of 1926 however, that negotiations were completed, and the School took possession of the land off Ilkeston Road. Work on laying out and levelling the land was to begin in February 1927, and the decision was made to no longer rent the recreation ground.

It was recognised that a toilet would be needed on the grounds (*'for the girls'*), but a changing room was not considered necessary. Fund-raising began to purchase a new pavilion at a cost of around £250, but it would be a number of years before this would be realised.

Throughout the 1920s, the 'Temporary Building' continued to receive very heavy use, particularly as the number of pupils rose. The 'Tin Tab' featured more than once in students' writings to the school magazine complaining about its dilapidated condition. In September 1920 the School took 60 more pupils than it had places for, hence the increase in staff referred to earlier. By the school year 1921/2, figures were 335 pupils, plus 26 'probationers' and nine student teachers. The School had ceased training pupil teachers the year before, but continued to have probationary teachers for 2½ days a week. At this point, senior pupils were allowed to use the mining laboratory, simply to give the school more space. The class for probationary teachers was closed at Christmas 1922, alleviating the situation slightly.

However, there was not going to be a constant increase in pupil numbers. At the annual speech day in December 1925 the Headmaster told the school that 111 children had left the previous July, and that there would now be a little more room. By the start of 1927/8, numbers had risen to 311, but by the following May had fallen back to 294 – the County advised the governors not to expect that staff vacancies would be filled unless numbers increased. The School had 16 full-time teachers, which gave a pupil-teacher ratio of 18.4:1 – very good by today's standards, and, as far as the County was concerned, too good! It is more than a possibility that, for fee-paying pupils especially, the recessions of the 1920s had more than a little part to play in the number and age of children leaving the school.

A lower wall to make the junction of Wilmot Street and Mundy Street easier to negotiate.

The decade did not see any major changes to the buildings, although in 1923 the School agreed to lower the wall at the junction of Wilmot Street and Mundy Street, so as to allow road users a better view. One place the governors wanted to keep from public view was the girls' playground. In 1922 the governors wrote to the Education Committee asking that the Wilmot Street gate be altered to stop people looking in when the gate was open. The Council's view was that the gate should be locked, or, '*if loiterers persisted in looking at the girls during their drill lessons'*, the police should be called! A far cry from today's high-security fencing around the majority of schools.

Its magazine also showed that the School was becoming more adventurous in organising out-of-school visits. The first one mentioned was to Haddon Hall in 1922. Then, in May 1924, Mr Stoddard took a group of 150 or so pupils to the Empire Exhibition at the Empire Stadium, Wembley. By the end of the decade, there had been two foreign trips recorded in the pages of the magazine, to Switzerland and to Paris, albeit for much smaller groups of students.

At the meeting of the governors on 15 May 1928, Ralph Stoddard announced his intention to retire on 31 December, after 35 years in office. The governors accepted his resignation with regret, adding that, *'They would miss him very much and all hoped he would have many years to enjoy his well-earned retirement.'*

The following month, Mr Stoddard's replacement, Mr F.L. Allan, classics master at the Royal Grammar School, Worcester, was announced. At the same meeting, Mr Stoddard reported that he had commissioned, subject to the governors' acceptance, the well known local artist, Mr Bissill, to paint four panels for the north side of the school hall. Mr Stoddard felt it was desirable that typical examples of mural decoration by Mr Bissill should be in the possession of the school, and he would be glad to present them. Mr Mayfield, chairman of the governors, expressed their willing and grateful acceptance of the offer.

George Bissill, around 1926.

And so began a long and apparently embittered saga with which to end Mr Stoddard's days at the school.

George W. Bissill was born in Fairford, Gloucestershire, in 1896, the son of a coal-miner from Langley Mill. By 1901 the family was back in the area, and

George went on to become a pupil at the Heanor Secondary and Technical School. After leaving school, no later than the age of 13, like so many other of his contemporaries, he became a miner. After six years, he then joined the forces and served in France from 1915 to 1918, where he suffered from the effects of gas attacks. Around 1920, he studied at the Nottingham School of Art for a short time. After that he moved to London, and for several years he worked as a pavement artist. His first one-man exhibition was at the Redfern Gallery in 1925, after which, according to an essay by an art critic 50 years later, *'Bissill-mania swept the country'*. His pictures can still be found in various galleries and museums; his early work has a very distinctive style, particularly when depicting life at the coalface. Bissill died in 1973, virtually forgotten.

So, as local Heanor artists go, Bissill was a major player. That, combined with the fact that he was an ex-pupil of the School, made him an ideal choice for Mr Stoddard. George Bissill was commissioned to paint four panels to represent *'Music, Art, Literature, and Science'*.

Mr Stoddard gave his final report at the annual speech day in December 1928. On behalf of the School, he was presented with a silver rose bowl, and his wife received a silver fruit bowl. In a separate presentation by the old students, which took place in January, he was presented with a bureau. Over 250 people attended the event.

In March 1929, three months after his retirement, the governors decided that they would like to view the panels, along with the area Education Officer, Mr Feek, and the county architect. After the viewing, in July 1929, a special meeting resolved that *'the Governors, after having viewed them, regret that they cannot see their way to accept the gift'*. No reason for this decision is recorded in the minutes.

Correspondence between the governors and their former Headmaster continued. Mr Stoddard wanted an expert to report on the paintings, but the County Education Officer advised the governors not to get involved in any form of enquiry as to their artistic merit.

Bissill's designs for *Music* and *Art*.

On 1 November 1929, the Ripley & Heanor News reported the indignation of the artist himself at the decision to reject the panels. The grounds apparently given to Bissill were that, '*some of the figures are indecent, the pictures are not fit to be exhibited in a children's school, and are not fit for the uplift of*

The *Science* and *Literature* panels.

education'. (To be fair to the governors, they always stressed that this was not the reason for their rejection of the paintings.)

In the meantime, Mr Stoddard had sought, and obtained, the support of an art expert, Miss A.M. Berry, whose letter was published in the Ripley and Heanor

News on 13 December. She stated that the paintings were *'admirably suited for the hall'*. They were designed to *'occupy a space between the balcony and the wainscotting'*. They would have been *'at right angles to the war memorial by the late Caley Robinson'*. Miss Berry found the decision of the governors to be incredible. She concluded with a note to Mr Stoddard to the effect that *'those who have seen the photographs of the panels find it difficult to believe that your gift, so worthy of enthusiastic acceptance, has been rejected'*.

The governors did not appear totally unanimous in their decision to reject the gift. At the December meeting Mr Stanley announced that he would ask for a vote on the subject at the next meeting – when it came to a vote, only three out of 14 governors were in favour of acceptance.

Later in December, Mr Stoddard loaned the paintings to the governors of the Heanor & District Memorial Hospital, of which he was the financial secretary. They were displayed in the town hall, with an entry fee going to support hospital funds. Hundreds attended to view the paintings – not surprising considering the amount of publicity generated.

In February 1930, the governors were asked for permission to hang the Bissill paintings in the school hall for inspection by Mr Claude Flight, R.B.A., prior to his giving a lecture at the town hall. This was so that the work could be judged *'in position in the Hall for which it was designed'*. Permission was given, but only for two hours at a weekend, when the school would be shut and nobody else would see them!

Following this, the story dropped out of the newspapers, and no further reference to these four paintings by Bissill has been found. However, during the preparation of this book, the author was contacted by the granddaughter of one of Bissill's close friends. She informed us that it is believed that Bissill finally destroyed the pictures following the School's rejection of them. However, photographs of the murals have been found, and it is therefore interesting to ponder how many of the readers of this book today will regard the paintings as *'indecent'*.

This was not, though, the end of the story. In 1934, Mr Stoddard tried again (though this time details seem to have been kept from the local press).

He wrote to the governors telling them that he had invited George Bissill to paint another four panels with a view to their being accepted for the School.

The nature of the designs was not disclosed, but he stressed that they would find these works *'attractive and dignified'*. This time, he had also arranged for the artist to submit designs for consideration by the governors prior to the work being completed. The governors agreed to *'tentatively accept the offer, subject to the proposed designs being submitted for their approval and also the Local Education Authority, and the first completed panel submitted for their inspection and approval before the others are proceeded with'*.

In March 1934, the governors viewed the proposed mural designs. They gave Mr Stoddard approval to go ahead and have one of the panels completed, but at this stage would not commit themselves to accepting the finished products. Copies of the designs were sent to the County Education Office, who replied later in the year that they had no objection, but did not wish to *'express any opinion as to the suitability of the panels for display in the assembly hall'*. The governors started to get cold feet again, and resolved to discuss with Mr Stoddard the *'desirability of an alternative offer'*.

In January 1935, the governors viewed a completed panel in the school hall. After doing so, they decided that *'a more suitable memorial to Mr Stoddard's long connection with the school would be more in uniformity with the standing and status of the school'*. They had rejected their former Headmaster's offer again! Mr Stoddard replied with a lengthy letter, complaining that the governors had allowed him to spend a considerable amount of money, and that they had given scant regard to Bissill's reputation. (Mr Stoddard pointed out that Bissill had recently been chosen by the Post Master General to carry out a painting to symbolise the work of the Post Office.) One expert, he quoted, had said that the new panels were *'too good to be tucked away in a country town'*. The explanation Mr Stoddard had been given for the governors' refusal of the murals was not, this time, on artistic, educational, or aesthetic grounds. Rather they wanted *'something more permanent'*. In view of this, in a last-ditch attempt to get them to accept the panels, Mr Stoddard added:

> *It has been an intention to establish a scholarship at the school in memory of our dear son Cyril. I have set aside £1,000 for the same. If you care to accept the panels and the scholarship as one gift, I am prepared to establish the scholarship at some not too distant date after the mural decorations are accepted and installed. To me it seems that to reject the offer of the panels alone would be a very unfortunate decision.*

The governors, however, thought otherwise, and even Mr Stoddard's offer of a gift of such significant value failed to persuade them. They informed him that they were not able to accept the panels. They did say that they would try to persuade the District Council to hang them in their new offices at Shanakiel. It is not known whether this was ever pursued, and no more is heard of Bissill or the murals in the minutes of the governors' meetings.

Instead of Ralph Stoddard's plans for an exciting set of contemporary murals in the assembly hall, the final selection for a memorial to the School's first Headmaster was unveiled in 1938 – a portrait of the man himself. Painted by Ernest Townsend of Derby, the portrait still hangs in the old hall today.

Mr Stoddard continued to play a major part in the life of the community, including the School, long after retirement, but his days of making the decisions were finished. After 35 years service, and after several major disagreements with the governors, it was they, not Mr Stoddard, who had the final say.

Chapter 7

The 1930s and the War Years

The departure of Ralph Stoddard was, undoubtedly, the 'end of an era'. It is also true to say that the school would not have the same degree of stability as regards the headmaster until the end of the story. Mr Stoddard had been at the school for 35 years; the next 28 years would see a total of five headmasters.

One immediate change (though possibly having nothing to do with the change of leadership) was the cover of the school magazine, which became bright orange in colour and incorporated the school crest on its front.

1929 School Magazines.

The new Head, Major Frederick Leonard Allan, was somewhat different from his predecessor. Mr Stoddard, having moved to Heanor from the People's College in Nottingham, had a scientific and technical background. Major Allan, however, had entirely different credentials. He had been educated at the Royal Grammar School, Newcastle, and Emmanuel College, Cambridge. Like so many of his generation, his university career was disrupted by the First

School prefects photograph 1933/4. Front row includes Mr White, head girl Dorothy Bostock, Headmaster Mr Allen, head boy F.H.Winchcomb, and Miss Webb. Other pupils featured are: Gladys Saint, Mary Pepper, Sybil Moore, R.Madeley, E.G.Thorpe, T.R.Jackson, J.W.H. Richardson, H.D.Freeman, and Ann Cope.

World War, and he was awarded a 'War Degree' in 1919; this was given on the basis of the work done for the Classical Tripos prior to enlisting. He went on to gain an MA from Cambridge in 1922. Prior to his appointment at Heanor, he had served as classics master at the Royal Grammar School in Worcester for six years. He must have found the move to Heanor quite dramatic; there was no long tradition of Latin, it being a subject offered at the age of 13 to those destined for university. A pupil at the time, writing his memories some 70 years later, recalled a definite change of pace in Latin lessons.

One task for the governors was to find suitable accommodation for the new Headmaster. Although there is no record of what the arrangements were, it is probable that Mr Stoddard's house had originally been provided by the School, as was the case with most Headmasters in the late nineteenth century. However, he retained possession of it until his death, and Mr Allan moved into The Dene, on Mansfield Road, just below the junction with Hands Road. The cost, £55 per annum, was met by the Education Committee. This house, which would be demolished for road-widening around 1935, had been the family home of the Victorian writer William Howitt (and, for a short time after their marriage, was also home to his wife Mary).

Beside the change in headmasters, the early years of the 1930s saw a couple of other notable departures. The chairman of the governors since 1921, Henry Boyce Mayfield, himself a former pupil, died in March 1932, and was replaced by Thomas Horsley. Mr Horsley had a long connection with education in the Heanor area, and was Headmaster of Langley Mill Boys' School. A retirement in the same year was that of William Rodway Barnes, art teacher at the School since 1898, and a considerable artist in his own right. It was Mr Barnes who designed the blazer-badge, initially a design for book-plates.

The year 1930 saw the inauguration of the Parents' Association, which continued its support and fund-raising for the School until the very end. Initially, fund-raising was still being dedicated primarily to the pavilion fund. The cost of the work had risen from the initial estimate of £250 to £600, and the County Education Office repeatedly refused to assist the School in funding the project. The Parent Association's 'Final Bazaar', in November 1931, raised a huge total of £350, enough for work to be started. Interestingly, the first day of the two-day event was opened by Mr Stoddard, while England cricketer R.W.V. Robins opened the second day.

The pavilion was formally opened on 13 September 1932 by Sir Julien Cahn, who brought a team of famous amateur cricketers, including two with Test Match credentials (Mr Robins and D.T.B. Morkel), to play a combined

Nottinghamshire and Derbyshire professional eleven, captained by old-boy, R.H. Wilson. Cahn's XI won by two wickets.

The 1932 pavilion.

Alongside the matter of the pavilion, another development had been taking place. Heanor Secondary School had moved a considerable way away from its original role as a technical school, and was now totally mainstream in its curriculum. There had been a need, in the 1890s, for a school which was dedicated to technical education, particularly in an area such as Heanor, with its emphasis on mining and industry. That need had not diminished, and this was recognised by the Education Department. As mentioned earlier, the purchase of the land for Heanor Secondary School to use as playing fields was also taken as an opportunity by the County to develop an additional establishment in the town – the Heanor Mining and Technical School.

The Mining School was established in 1930, and in 1934 extensions to its buildings more than doubled its size; by 1937 it had over 300 students. Qualifications were attained by students not only in mining subjects, but also in mechanical and electrical engineering, in building and construction, and in secretarial skills. From its very outset, the 1930/31 prospectus for the College, included the 'Secondary School Evening Institute', which was organised by

Mr Hosegood at the School. Despite this, the two units did not always see eye to eye; the School, which had fought so hard for its playing fields, would on occasions refuse requests from the Mining College to use them. But, with the odd exception such as this, the relationship between the two was good, and forty years later, the co-operation between these two very different establishments was to feature in discussions on the School's future.

Heanor Mining College.

H.M. Inspectors again carried out a visit to the School in 1934, and again were very favourably impressed, reporting that it was *'greatly improved since the last visit'*. Their only real criticisms concerned the lack of a gymnasium, and inadequate library provision. In the July 1934 edition of the school magazine, the editors comment on improvements to the grounds of the school:

> *At the Boys' end of the School grounds, where there used to be an expanse of brick-ends and tin cans..., there now stretch spacious lawns, complete with weather station; several trees have died of old age, but not so the Temporary Building – that venerable pile...*

Alterations had been made to the interior of the 'Tin Tab', which meant that it was looking forward to many more years of *'Tin-Tabernacular temporariness'*. The HMI report explained that the building was now being used to accommodate three classrooms and a biology laboratory.

A 1930s view of the School from Ilkeston Road, showing the 'Tin Tab'. Note how the main road turned left into Mundy Street at this time.

This same magazine also reported what the governors had been informed in May, namely that Mr Allan had submitted his resignation, and would be leaving after the summer break. Mr Allan had been at the School for just 5½ years – indeed, the saga of Mr Stoddard's gift to the School was still continuing at this time. Mr Allan's departure was to take on the role of Headmaster at Wallasey Grammar School, a position which was regarded as a definite promotion. At a presentation by the Parents' Association in June, the chairman, Mr T.J. Lewis, praised the leaving Headmaster, stating that *'the school's prestige had increased considerably during Mr Allan's term of office'*.

Mr Allan's replacement was Mr Thomas Percival Spencer, who was the Headmaster of the County Secondary School at Eckington in north Derbyshire, a not dissimilar establishment. His educational background was more 'red-brick', with a BA in History from the University of Manchester. Mr Spencer was unable to take up the post until November 1934, so Mr White deputised for the start of the term.

Heanor Secondary School staff, 1935.
Rear: H.L.Harlow, Miss Grimwood, J.Hancock, C.O.Betts, H.G.Sears, Miss Harbour, G.F.Hosegood, J.Taylor.
Front: V.Youle, Miss Davis, Miss Winfield, A.J.White, T.P.Spencer, Miss Webb, Miss Gibbon, Miss Bolton, Miss Dawson.

At the same time that the end of the arguments over George Bissill's pictures was reached, another old perennial issue was finally reaching fruition. At the governors meeting in February 1935, they again resolved to ask for electric lighting. And this time they got it, 14 years after the first request. Furthermore, when it was installed towards the end of the year, the County also gave provision for lighting in the pavilion, by taking it from the adjacent Mining School.

It has been mentioned earlier that there had always been a problem with pupils leaving the school earlier than planned. In 1935, the School Certificate became a five-year course, with students normally taking it at the age of 16, two years beyond school leaving age. By sending their children to Heanor Secondary School, parents committed to keep them there for four years, and whilst the majority kept to this commitment, there was a tendency for some children to leave early unless they were going to be teachers. Until the school leaving age was increased, this would continue to cause problems. Local employers were, as far as the School was concerned, partly to blame for this issue. The County Council itself was a culprit, for in October 1935, the governors wrote to them in protest over a recent advertisement for a junior post. Applications were restricted to those between the ages of 14 and 16, which meant that anyone who had stayed at a secondary school for the full term was precluded from applying. Similarly, in 1937, a strongly worded letter was sent to the Ripley Co-operative Society asking them not to take on scholars from the school until they had finished their allotted course.

Partly to combat this problem, another important feature of this time was the loan fund, to which the Parents' Association had turned its attention after the success of the pavilion. The prime aim of the fund, as Mr Spencer explained, was to help those students *'about to leave or recently having left school who would find it difficult to raise the necessary money for examination fees, or for the whole cost of some training not subsidised by any authority'*. By the time the December 1937 magazine was published, they were able to give details of the loan fund. A maximum of £15 was available per pupil upon leaving the School, the Headmaster was to deal with applications, and each loan had to be guaranteed by two or more persons, who agreed to pay the loan back if the applicant defaulted after starting work. Other fund-raising was also directed towards helping students with expenses for the growing number of sporting activities.

The period between the wars, and the 1930s especially, was probably the heyday of clubs and societies at the school, certainly if the school magazine was a reflection of activities. There was an active dramatic society, a literary society, historical and geographical societies, a sketch club, a natural history society, the League of Nations union, which had regular meetings discussing current international affairs, and *Le Circle Français*. The School had its own Girl Guide company (and later a cadet corps), and on the charity front a Barnardo Helpers' League ran for many years, as did the Zenana Missionary Society. Sports teams were equally popular, with hockey, cricket, tennis and football all featuring very regularly in the pages of the magazines.

Aerial photograph from the 1930s.

It was almost certainly during this period that the school hymn was designated. The school magazine had suggested a search for a 'school song' as early as March 1929, but this was not commented upon further, and at that time the annual speech day commenced with the singing of *Jerusalem*. The closest that the School had to having a school song (as opposed to a hymn) appears to have been the annual singing of *Forty Years On* (by John Farmer), on the last day of summer term. This tradition certainly took place throughout the 1930s and into the 1940s, but appears to have ended with the Second World War. There is no record of when *To be a Pilgrim* became the school hymn, but a newspaper report in November 1938, referring to speech day, stated that the *'proceedings opened with the singing of the school Hymn "He who would valiant be"'*. This is, so far, the earliest known reference to it. The decision to have a school hymn would, for the time, have been a natural step in the development of school traditions, a more 'corporate identity'.

From the late 1930s, another war appeared inevitable, and preparations began for it. By the end of 1938, first aid classes were now being run by the Police and St John Ambulance in the Temporary Building at weekends and in the evenings, and the local ARP Committee was looking at the School as a possible de-contamination centre should it be required. By the spring of 1939, the Territorial Army was using the school and its grounds two evenings a week for training. The April 1939 magazine reported on the *'clashing of knitting needles'* throughout the School, as the girls made blankets for refugees.

The 1936 Education Act had provided for the raising of the school leaving age from 14 to 15 from September 1939. In the event, this was cancelled, and the provision had to wait a further eight years. War was declared against Germany on 3 September 1939, but this took nobody by surprise.

The County Emergency Committee had forbidden the opening of the School after the summer holiday until it had *'adequate protection'*, which was to be provided by trenches around the School. In the meantime, the 338 pupils on the register were being set homework, and staff were employed to correct it. School re-opened a month late, on 9 October. The governors declared that full fees still had to be paid by parents, as the School's expenditure had remained the same. In recompense for the missed classes, there were to be reduced Christmas and Easter breaks.

Wartime precautions were to remain a feature of school life for several years. By the time of the December 1939 magazine, the editors wrote that it already seemed so long ago that they didn't have to carry gas masks to school. Hardest hit by the war were the societies and sports. All external fixtures were cancelled, and most of the societies were unable to meet. The 3rd Heanor Cadets, based in the School under the captainship of Miss Webb, were working for the war-effort; each member who lived in Heanor carried out five hours duty a week staffing the phones at the fire station during the evenings.

To make matters worse, February 1940 saw extremely severe weather. For over four weeks, roads were impassable due to heavy snow, buses and trains were cancelled, school attendance was erratic, and all sport was impossible. But as the year progressed, and there had been no invasion, some semblance of normality returned. School societies and sports were almost back to normal, though inter-school matches, except with the neighbouring schools of Stainsby and Ilkeston, were still cancelled because of the difficulties and dangers of travelling. (Stainsby Hall, in Smalley, had been taken over by St Aloysius College, from Highgate, London, whose pupils were evacuated there – it was known as Stainsby House School. Local, fee-paying, pupils were accepted too, and it continued beyond the war years.)

The wartime minutes of the governors reveal the day-to-day privations caused by the war. The domestic science room was ear-marked for feeding people whose homes might be destroyed by enemy action. The School's cycle sheds were taken over by the ARP Committee as part of the School's shelters. The ARP's case was, no doubt, all the stronger since the chief air raid warden for the town was the Headmaster, Mr Spencer. Even more than the usual number of pupils were leaving school before they were 16. Petrol for the school lawnmowers was in short supply, and had to be taken from the County pumps, rather than using the local garage (Mr Marchbank's), and the School was not allowed to recruit a boy to assist the groundsman during the summer, as had been standard practice. Even the layout of the school playing field had to be considered in relation to its possible use as a landing strip for enemy aircraft; it was perhaps for this reason that parts of the playing fields were cultivated for a potato crop. Several of the staff (Mr Betts, Mr Hosegood and Mr Taylor) enlisted for the Army Officers Emergency Reserve, and the School knew that it could lose their services without notice if they were required. The School received its first evacuees in November 1940. Senior pupils were now taught first aid and fire practice, the Head arranged for the purchase of camp beds for staff on fire-watch duty at night, along with ladders to reach the roof in case of incendiary bombs. First the playground and then the playing fields were used for drill practice by the army training corps. But, for pupils, perhaps the biggest loss was that the summer holiday in 1940 was reduced to just two weeks.

Elsewhere, the School's efforts in providing comforts for old students serving in the forces, along with other charitable work and fund-raising, were similar to those during the previous war. The School also helped 'Dig for Victory', with not only potatoes on the playing fields, but also cabbages in the school gardens.

The autumn term in 1940 saw the pupils having to use the air-raid shelters twice for real air-raids, though the comment in the December school magazine was that the biggest worry was *'the danger of getting back in time for a French test'*! The nearest the School came to receiving an enemy hit, however, was when a bomb landed on the boys' playing field.

Until December 1941, the school magazine had continued as normal, with three editions each year in December, April and July. The impact of the war, however, meant that the publication now dropped to a single annual edition, starting in July 1942, and much reduced in size. This edition reported the departure, after eight years in post, of Mr Spencer who moved to take on the position of Headmaster at the Burnage High School for Boys in Manchester.

Mr A.J. White, who had been at the school for 37 years, took on the responsibility of Acting Headmaster for the first term of 1942/3 until Mr Spencer's replacement could start. For this task, he received an extra payment of £35. The new Headmaster was appointed at the start of 1943; John Edmund Simpson, who was a graduate of Corpus Christi, Cambridge, and a former geography master, moved from his post as principal of Scarborough College. He was destined to be the shortest serving Head in the history of the School.

Inevitably, the war saw the death of a number of old students in action. The first to be recorded in the school magazine, in December 1940, was that of Sergeant Alfred White, of the R.A.F. By the end of the war, the total number of old boys killed reached 24, including a former head boy, Captain F.L. Shears. The war years also saw the death, in 1942, of Mrs Apame Stoddard, wife of the first Head. Whatever problems the staff may have had with Mrs Stoddard in the 1910s, the list of mourners at her funeral shows that these had clearly long since been put aside.

While families throughout the area suffered their personal losses, the School itself, and Heanor in general, came through the war unscathed. With an end to war in sight, the country started to prepare for change. One of these changes was to be the Education Act of 1944.

School hockey team, 1944/5.
Rear: Rene Hartley, Marian Belfield, Valerie Longden, Margot Wright, Dorothy McGowan, Dorothy Ball, Helen Fletcher, Molly Stanley. Front: Betty Fletcher, Kathleen Walker, Mr J.E.Simpson, Jean Hamilton, Miss E.Gibbon, Glenis Gunn, Dorothy Hartley.

Chapter 8

Heanor Grammar School 1945 - 1957

The Education Act of 1944 (or the Butler Act, as it was widely known) was to cause major changes to the education system nationally. Heanor, of course, was no different. The Act, which was never fully implemented, ensured that no fees could be charged for admission to, or for the provision of education at, any School maintained by a Local Education Authority.

Prior to the Act, Heanor Secondary School had still operated the original system. Pupils had been taken mainly at the age of 11 years; some came to the School on a free scholarship, after qualifying for this by a form of examination, while others paid for the privilege. Children who did not attend the Secondary School went to one of the several elementary schools in the area, where they stayed until the age of 14.

The new Act saw the school leaving age rise to 15, a provision which was implemented in April 1947. (The Act actually gave the government the power to raise school leaving age to 16, but it was nearly 30 years before this happened.) At the same time, the Act introduced new types of secondary education. The secondary modern school was created, along with technical schools and grammar schools, entry to the latter being by selection by an exam which became known as the 'eleven-plus'. Elementary schools were now designated as primary schools, and pupils stayed at them until the age of 11. These changes did not happen overnight, and as late as 1957 there were still elementary schools in the area which took children up to the age of 14.

In March 1945, the governors of Heanor Secondary School, which was already selective, recommended that its name be changed to Heanor Grammar School. The change appears to have taken place immediately, and the July magazine for that year shows the new title on its cover. (The magazine was still a thin annual publication, due to the shortages caused by the war – twice yearly publication, in the spring and summer terms, commenced in 1947.)

Until the 1940s, the School had normally taken two forms (60 pupils) each year. The system required the new Grammar School to expand. In 1944, three forms (90 pupils) were admitted, and the plan was to have two and three-form admission in alternate years, before changing to a full three-form entry after a few years. Needless to say, the immediate impact of this change was that the

Temporary Building was going nowhere! Indeed, the School started planning for additional buildings. The 'Tin Tab' was renamed 'Block A', and was joined at the start of 1950 by 'Block B', situated on the Ilkeston Road edge of the site. This, too, was meant to be a temporary fixture, a HORSA building (an acronym for *Hutting Operation for the Raising of School leaving Age*), which comprised three classrooms, a cloakroom, and a tiny office used by the school secretary, along with lavatories. At the same time, work was ongoing at the opposite side of the school, next to Wilmot Street, on improving the kitchen and dining facilities.

These were all regarded as stopgap measures; it was recognised that the School needed a more permanent extension if it was to cope with increased numbers. The problem with the site of the School was that it was on an 'island', surrounded by roads with other buildings on the opposite side. Extension was not going to be as easy as for many other schools in the area. However, the School did not occupy the island alone. The Heanor Urban District Council still had possession of a number of buildings opposite the church, and also the fire station on Wilmot Street. Discussions began in 1947 in an attempt to acquire the land owned by Heanor UDC, a total of 2,701 square yards. Initial approaches to the Council were not successful, as they had earmarked the land for a new post office. A specific request for a lease on the fire station was refused in 1950, but in January 1951 the County Planning Committee agreed that the land adjacent to the School would be reserved for educational purposes. However, it would be a few years before this was developed, and in the meantime, the school continued to be cramped.

Another, perhaps unexpected, impact of the new system, which must have caused a shift in the School's character, was a significant change in the ratio of the sexes. In 1942, there were 142 girls and 201 boys enrolled. By 1950, the numbers were 222 girls and 208 boys. In the pre-war system, the majority of pupils had to pay to attend the School. Now places were free for all. The explanation for the change undoubtedly lay in the then perceived (by some) lack of benefit in paying for a girl's education, at a time when many parents would have expected their daughters to work for a few years at most, and then marry and stay at home. Society, and its view on women at work, was to change dramatically over the next fifty years, but in the 1940s, this was still far away.

Another issue concerning the increase in pupil numbers was the annual speech day. Quite simply, the school hall was not big enough to cope, and in 1947 the decision was made to hold two separate speech days, one for the juniors and another for the seniors. The hall was filled to capacity for each event!

The end of the war brought the opportunity to develop the school more aesthetically. As early as April 1945 discussions were taking place on landscaping the gardens. The railings which featured in the earlier photographs of the School had now gone, no doubt as part of the war effort. But vandalism was less of a problem in those days, and the flower-beds at the front of the School were then, and for many years later, lovingly tended to shape the letters HGS in flowers. The condition of the gardens was so '*excellent*' in 1950 that the governors wrote to the gardener, Mr Baldwick, to congratulate him. In 1949, work was carried out to level the playing field, so allowing the provision of an additional football pitch. This proved particularly useful since the Old Students Football Club, formed in May 1947, were using the field every other weekend. (The Old Students team played for a number of years, and then dwindled – the team was resurrected in the early 1960s and again used the School's grounds for matches.) The academic year 1949/50 also saw the restoration of the mural paintings by Caley Robinson in the School Hall. Mr Bladen, of Derby College of Art, carried out the restoration with advice from Professor Tristram.

The time following the end of the war also saw a number of significant staff changes. In January 1945, Mr Simpson, the Headmaster, was ordained as a priest by the Bishop of Derby at a service at Heanor Parish Church, and at the end of the year, he left to become the vice-principal of St. Paul's College, Cheltenham. His tenure of office was exactly three years.

Other departures in the second half of the 1940s included the senior master, Mr A.J. White, who retired in the summer of 1945 after 40 years at the school. 'Jimmy' White was not, unfortunately, to have a long retirement. His death was reported in the school magazine in spring 1948; in the 1953 magazine, it was announced that the old students had donated an oak candlestick for Marlpool Church in his memory. Chemistry teacher Mr C.G. ('Billy') Betts, who had started at the School in 1920, now took the senior master post. Following Mr Simpson's departure, Mr Betts stood in as Acting Headmaster until the new Head, Mr William E. Egner, who at the time was with the Air Ministry, could start at the beginning of the summer term, 1946. A new search

Heanor Grammar School prefects, 1947.
Back: Ivy Clay, Jean Howarth, John Banton, George Wedd, Max Payne, Mike Hancock, Christine Gibbs, Eileen Sisson.
Front: Joy Brookes, Mr Betts, Dorothy Hartley (head girl), Mr Egner, Ross Hesketh (head boy), Miss Webb, Peter Mellors.

for accommodation for the Headmaster commenced (it is not known where Mr Spencer and Mr Simpson had resided). After considering The Starthe, off Hands Road, a seven-year lease was taken out for the new Headmaster on The

Chestnuts, on Mundy Street, at the end of 1945, but the lease was terminated in 1950.

Former pupil, Mr H.V. Youle, who had been teaching English since 1919, left at the end of 1945, due to ill health. Mrs Brown (formerly Miss Buswell) left at the same time, after ten years as art mistress, to take up a post at Derby Art School. The illness and subsequent death of the school cook, Mrs Brewin, who had been with the School since 1931, also added to the list of departures in 1946. Easter 1948 saw the retirement of Miss Ellen H. Webb, after almost 34 years at the school. She had been appointed as French mistress in 1914, and subsequently became senior mistress. She took an active part in the School's activities throughout her career, running the Guides and Young Helpers' League (Dr. Barnado's Homes). She was shortly followed by Miss Ellen Gibbon, who retired in the summer of 1948, after thirty years at the School. Another departure that year was that of the school caretaker, Mr Rose, who had been in post for 28 years.

With so many long-serving staff members leaving, it is perhaps right also to look at some of the staff who were now joining the School. Mrs Edith Brookes became school secretary in December 1945, a post she would hold until 1964. Mr Howard ('Harry') F. Houldsworth joined the School in September 1947, as German teacher, and would remain at the School for the rest of its existence. The post of senior mistress and senior foreign languages mistress was, on the retirement of Miss Webb, taken by a new arrival at the school in 1948, Miss Vera Pugsley, who would remain there for 14 years. In 1949 there was an influx of new staff: Mr W.H. ('Jigger') Johnson (geography) would stay at the school until 1973, while Mr John Diggle (boys' crafts) and Mr Edward H. ('Jerry') Jerome (French), would be in post until the end. Another arrival in 1949, albeit only for a few years, was Mrs G.W. 'Betty' Redgate, teaching girls' PE; as Miss Severn, she had been the head girl in 1942/3, and had subsequently married the head boy of that year.

In 1946, the School formed a Parent-Staff Association, the successor to the previously successful Parents' Association which had done so much to raise funds for the School since the days of the pavilion fund. The inaugural meeting took place in December, with a healthy attendance of more than 100 parents. The list of committee members is interesting for it shows how the catchment area for the School had changed over the years, as each member represented a geographical area. There were two representatives for Heanor itself, and one for Langley Mill and Aldercar, one for Langley and Marlpool, one for Loscoe and Denby, and one for Smalley. The two remaining ones are of most significance, for Mr Rowe represented the district of Pinxton, a village quite some distance away from Heanor (this situation lasted until 1950, when Pinxton fell within the catchment area of Swanwick Hall Grammar School). The final one was the representative for Nottinghamshire; the School had always had a steady, albeit not large, number of pupils from over the border, and this shows that the arrangement still continued for a while after the restructuring of secondary education. (A number of pupils from Nottinghamshire continued to attend the School until as late as 1964.)

The 1946 edition of the school magazine reported on the impossibility of keeping the Old Students' Association active during the war, other than the occasional football or hockey match. However, a revival began as soon as the war was over. Subscription cost members 2/6d. a year, and the first act of the reformed group had been to present a retirement gift to Mr White. The

The Second World War memorial, in place on the stage in the school hall.

Committee then set upon compiling a roll of honour for those past students who had lost their lives in the war. Press notices were issued in a number of publications, in an attempt to trace the names of those eligible to be listed.

A meeting of the O.S.A., along with parents, governors and staff, in November 1947, agreed to provide a memorial in the form of a reading desk, bearing a plaque inscribed with the names of the fallen, a chair and a lectern. These items were all crafted in oak, bearing the Derbyshire coat of arms, and were carved by a Heanor man, Mr B. Dorrington. In addition, there was also a book of remembrance. Fund-raising was a laborious process, but the memorial was finally dedicated at a service on Empire Day, May 1949. The service was conducted by Mr Egner, the memorial was dedicated by an old pupil, Rev. Douglas Jephson of Riddings, and former Headmaster Mr Spencer, still Head at Burnage School, was also in attendance.

On 29 August 1949, Ralph Stoddard died at Heanor Memorial Hospital, after a very short illness, aged 82 years. At the time of his death, he was writing a *Review of the Early History of Heanor Grammar School*, which was subsequently published. As well as being the Head of the School for 35 years, Mr Stoddard had played a very major role in the community. He had been treasurer and later secretary of the Memorial Hospital, prior to its nationalisation in 1948. He was one of the founders of the Heanor Carnival, and was on the War Memorial Park Committee. He was also a past Master of the Mundy Grove Lodge of the Freemasons and President of the English Bowling Association. At his funeral, not surprisingly, *He Who Would Valiant Be* was sung.

The school magazine becomes *The Heanorian*, changing design twice in a few years.

The last edition of the school magazine before Mr Stoddard's death saw a major change, and one that would last to the present day. The title was now *The Heanorian*. The editorial stated that the name, '*doesn't sound very euphonious, but we've heard worse, and it does suggest some connection with Heanor, even to a moderate intelligence*'. The aim to publish twice a year failed (except in the following year, 1950/51), and the magazine remained an annual publication until its demise.

While the name of the magazine was relatively simple to change, the name of the School was going to be as big a problem as in the past (and this continued until its final closure). By March 1949, the Education Committee was asking that the School revert to its old name, something which the governors preferred not to do. The discussions continued awhile, and in January 1950, the School was told that the Department of Education could not agree to their retaining the word 'Grammar' in the name. 'Heanor School' was considered as an option, but it does not appear that this suggestion was progressed any further at that time. In 1956, it was stated that the School was to be known as the 'Heanor County Secondary School', and that this name should be used in all correspondence with the Education Authority. At some time its official name was the 'Heanor Secondary Mixed (Grammar) School', and by 1976 the School was officially just 'Heanor School'. Not that any of this actually had any impact on the staff or pupils – in fact nobody other than the L.E.A. and the governors took any notice. To everyone in the community itself, the School remained 'The Grammar' from 1945 onwards.

Mr Egner left Heanor at the end of 1950, after just 4½ years, in order to take up the post of Headmaster at Ormskirk Grammar School, Lancashire. He was replaced by Mr Eric Clucas Sykes, a 44-year-old graduate of Liverpool University who taught music. The list of other notable departures and arrivals continued into the 1950s. In 1950, Mr Alec H. Lawley joined the English department, a post he would hold for the rest of the life of the school. In 1952 Miss E.M. Lovely replaced Mrs Redgate for girls' PE, Mr Walter Savage joined the school as part-time music teacher, a post which later became full-time and which he held until 1972, and Mr George F. Hosegood retired as senior maths master, after 32 years service. In 1953, Mr 'Spec' Harlow retired after 38 years as a maths teacher at the School at which he was first a pupil. While best remembered for his teaching, he was also a keen photographer; most of the photographs in the school magazine in the early 1950s were taken by him, and he continued providing this service for several years after retirement. Also retiring in 1953 was the school gardener, Mr Baldwick, who was almost 80 years of age. Two long-serving teachers retired in 1955: Miss Marjorie Dawson, who had taught English at the School since 1920, and Mr H.G. ('Toler') Sears, geography master since 1921. They were joined the following year by Mr J. ('Joey') Hancock, himself a former pupil at Heanor, who had taught physics since 1920; Mr Hancock also took an active role in the musical side of the School. Finally, two other new arrivals, both in the maths department were Mr Sidney Bailey (1955) and Mr George R. Dickie (1956).

Staff photograph, 1952.
Back: D.L. Hind, A.H. Lawley, D.L.G. Jenkins, J. Diggle, K.C. Joslin, W. Savage.
Middle: E.H. Jerome, Mrs Brookes, G.I. Walters, Miss M.C. Currie, H.F. Houldsworth, W.H. Johnson, Miss H. Twiss, M. Osborne, Miss E.M. Lovely, F.V. Mills.
Front: H.G. Sears, Miss D. Mee, H.L. Harlow, Miss M.L. Winfield, C.G. Betts, E.C. Sykes, Miss V. Pugsley, G.F. Hosegood, Miss M. Dawson, J. Hancock, Miss E. Wallis.

Both would be at the School until its closure (albeit that Mr Dickie took a few years away from the School in the 1960s).

In 1951, the examination system changed nationally. School leaving age had already been increased to 15, but pupils at schools such as Heanor Grammar School were expected to stay on at least until the age of 16, when they would take the School Certificate. Those who intended moving on to higher education would then need a further two years in order to sit the Higher School Certificate, normally in three subjects, with one additional subsidiary subject. (Is the idea of studying four or five AS-levels, followed by three A-levels, a reinvention of the wheel?) In June 1951 pupils took the General Certificate of Education for the first time, at either Ordinary or Advanced Level. Initially, grades were not awarded, and pupils simply passed or failed. School results were of a high standard throughout the period. In 1956, for example, a year in which there were two forms taking exams, 44 pupils obtained passes in five or more subjects at O-level, with 12 passing in eight subjects; the rest of the year had three or four O-level passes. Nowadays, this is a common occurrence, but not so in the 1950s.

Partly to fit in with the new structure, during the early 1950s, the School split its examination classes into three separate courses. So, in examination year, Class 5L would have its emphasis on arts and languages, Class 5S would specialise more on maths and science, while Class 5G would take a general approach.

The first HMI inspection since 1934 took place in 1952. Their report did not give any significant information, although, as usual, they commented on the accommodation being *'somewhat below present day requirements'*; they also added a perhaps veiled criticism in relation to the quality of teaching at the School, stating, *'there is room for more enterprise and sparkle'*. In the Headmaster's report later that year, Mr Sykes reported that there were now only 30 pupils in the sixth form, an issue which he blamed on the fact that *'everything is now free'*.

In 1953, the School celebrated its golden jubilee. The year started on a sad note though, with the death of the long-serving chairman of the governors, Thomas Horsley, after 21 years in the post. As well as this role, Mr Horsley had been the Headmaster of Langley Mill Boys' School from 1897 to 1939, and was perhaps the leading citizen in Langley Mill in his era. The year saw the introduction of a Latin motto, *Animo et Fide* ('*by courage and faith*'), beneath the school badge. At the same time, the badge was now in a plain rather than ornate shield. This featured not only on school blazers, but also on

The new school badge with the Latin motto, alongside the badge of the School before it was renamed a grammar school.

the front of The Heanorian. As part of the celebrations, there was a service at Heanor St. Lawrence's, attended by former Headmasters Mr Allan and Mr Spencer – and all the clergy taking part in the service were old boys. Another feature of the anniversary was the inclusion in the school magazine of two articles from old students, recalling their early days at the School. The authors were H.L. Harlow, the retiring maths teacher who started at Heanor in 1905, and H.H. Dix, of Smalley, who had started at the 'Tec' in 1895. Both have been quoted elsewhere in this work.

Of course, the year also saw national celebrations to commemorate the crowning of the new Queen. The Local Education Authority gave each school 2/- per pupil in order to provide a lasting memento of the occasion. The vast majority of schools used this money to purchase commemorative mugs, etc., which can still be found relatively easily. Heanor Grammar School, however, decided that rather than purchase items to be given to individual pupils, they would use the money to buy a new trophy, to be called the 'Coronation Trophy'. This would be awarded to the house (Ray, Flamstead, or Howitt – still the same system as in 1913) which gained the highest number of points for '*Games, Athletic Sports and Academic Work*'. It was hoped that this would form '*a more lasting reminder of the Coronation year than 400 beakers or spoons*'.

The post-war status of the School, and the boom in pupil numbers, made this period one of the strongest in extra-curricular activities. A glance at The Heanorian between 1954 and 1956 showed reports from various clubs and societies: the geographical society, the Girl Guides, the sketch club, the chess club, the English folk and American square dancing team, the literary and debating society, and S.P.Q.R. (the Latin society). Some of these were short-lived, but something new always popped up to take the place of clubs which folded. In his report at the 1956 speech day, Mr Sykes even remarked on the setting up of a photographic society – it is doubtful that he had ever read the 1909 school magazine, for if he had, he would have known that this was not a first!

This period also saw the formation and development of a school orchestra and school choir, and the early steps taken in this direction in the late 1940s were consolidated under the leadership of Mr Sykes, himself a keen musician (he was the deputy organist at Heanor Church). The first permanent school choir was set up with the arrival of a new music teacher, Miss Callin, in 1948, and the annual carol concert became established as a firm favourite in the town's calendar. The development of a school orchestra had been first mentioned in 1947, but this was a gradual and long term project, particularly in view of the cost of instruments – fund-raising was still continuing as late as 1955. Summer musical concerts began in 1949, and in 1950 a concert was held in aid of the Marlpool Church reconstruction fund (the church had burned down on Christmas Eve 1949). Although Miss Callin only stayed at the School for three years, her work was continued and substantially developed by Mr Savage, who became full-time in 1956, assisted by visiting music teachers, as well other interested staff members in their own time. During the 1950s, several pupils went on to a full time career in music. The School's commitment to music was firmly established, and the tradition was maintained until its closure.

Music was not the only performing art under the spotlight. The 1930s had seen a number of school drama productions, and these resumed at the end of the 1940s with the formation of a dramatic society. Productions in the ten years after the end of the war included: *The Importance of Being Earnest* (1947), *The Admirable Crichton* (1948), *Quiet Weekend* (1949), *I'll Leave it to You* (1950) (directed by Miss Pugsley), *I have Five Daughters* (1951), *Lady Precious Stream* (1952), *Mansfield Park* (1954), and *The Vicar of Wakefield* (1955). The post-war era was certainly the heyday of drama at Heanor Grammar School.

Sport also gathered momentum. Throughout the 20s, 30s and 40s, the sporting references in the school magazines were regular, but covered only football, cricket, hockey, occasionally tennis, and, of course, the annual sports day. The post-war period, however, saw the variety of sports mentioned increase considerably. In 1948, for the first time since the First World War, we are told that a number of pupils had received swimming certificates in the previous year. With swimming being a summer term event only, there was a *'dry-land class'* planned for boys wishing to take the bronze medallion. An inter-house swimming gala at Langley Baths is featured two years later. In 1951, an article by a third former explained the delights of going on the bus for a swimming session in the *'freezing'* pool at Langley. The School's cross-country running team was featured the following year, and there was a successful team for several years. In March 1950, the first girls' gymnastic competition was held. A badminton club was set up in December 1950, restricted to fifth and sixth formers, though badminton had featured occasionally in the Old Students' Association pages of the magazine over the years. The 1951 magazine also reported the formation of a boys' gym club and a boys' hockey club; Rugby Union was also offered, though only for a short time, to try to provide an alternative to soccer and cross-country. Final additions to the sporting options were mentioned in 1955, with plans for fencing and table tennis clubs.

In 1953, the School had become fully three-form entry, with around 90 new pupils each year. This saw a further dramatic rise in numbers, from 433 in 1952, 468 in 1953, 507 in 1954, and peaking at 540 in 1956. Still there had been no significant extension to the building. In his annual report at the 1954 speech day, Mr Sykes commented,

> *When I first came here I cast longing eyes on the valuable land behind the School which houses a muddle of semi-derelict buildings, set in and around what has been called the Council Yard. Of these buildings, one is actually the original Chemistry Lab.*

Discussions were still continuing between the L.E.A. and the District Council over land for future growth, but Mr Sykes was not to see this come to fruition.

Staff Photograph, 1956. Back row: G.R. Dickie, D.L.G. Jenkins, S. Bailey, A.L. Cooil, J. Diggle.
2nd row: A.H. Lawley, D.R. Fryer, W. Savage, R. Davy, Mrs C. Kosohorsky, M. Osborne, K.C. Joslin.
3rd row: Miss M. Longbottom, D.L. Hind, Mrs E. Brookes, W.H. Johnson, Miss M.E. Boreham, F.V. Mills, Miss E.M. Loveley, E.H. Jerome.
Front row: Miss T.G. Thicke, G.I. Walters, Miss M.L. Winfield, C.G. Betts, E.C. Sykes, Miss V. Pugsley, J. Hancock, Miss M. Wilford, H.F. Houldsworth.

102

On 11 November 1956, Mr Eric Clucas Sykes died at Heanor Memorial Hospital, aged just 51 years. He had gone into hospital for a routine operation, and his death was totally unexpected. He left a vacancy yet again for the regularly changing post of Headmaster. But the next Head would be staying for a while!

Chapter 9

Expansion and Preparation for Change, 1957 - 1964

Whilst this book is strictly a history of Heanor Grammar School, its development cannot be considered in isolation. This is particularly so from the mid-1950s onwards.

We have already seen how the Education Act of 1944 set out a proposed structure for secondary education which was gradually developing into reality in the Heanor area. A new secondary modern school had been opened at Aldercar in 1955. It would be several years before it would be able to cater for all the pupils designated to attend, but 440 started on its first day. It was designed to cater, once complete, for all pupils from the age of 11 to 15 years who had not been selected to attend the Grammar School. However, in line with the comprehensive ethos, from the first the new school also catered for those wanting to take O-levels at the age of 16, giving an additional year after the end of compulsory education. Nine of the pupils who started at Aldercar in 1955, at the age of 13, took O-levels in 1958. The Grammar School now had some competition!

Elsewhere in the area, pupils continued to attend the older schools (now retitled 'Secondary Modern') at Heanor Howitt and Codnor, until a second new school could be built in the area. The fact that they were housed in former elementary schools had some adverse effect on their status in the eyes of the local population, but nevertheless they achieved significant success. Heanor Aldercar Secondary Modern School was considerably larger than Heanor Grammar School (in 1959, by the time the School was fully complete, the comparative figures were 850 pupils at Aldercar compared with 540 at the Grammar School). It was also on a 'green field' site, rather than a town centre island. The same would be the case when Heanor Gate School opened in 1964. For these reasons alone, the next decade was going to see major changes in the education system in the area. Though, as we shall see, the biggest driving force was actually political ideology.

But before the changes, there was unfinished work to be carried out.

Following the untimely death of Mr Sykes, Mr Betts again carried out the role of Acting Headmaster until a replacement could be found. The new Head was Geoffrey R. Stone, a modern languages graduate of Manchester University, who had held a commission in the Intelligence Corps during the war, and was now working as a government inspector of schools in Northern Ireland. As a civil servant, he only had to give three months' notice, unlike teachers who could only change posts at the end of a term. And so, unusually for a new headmaster, he arrived at Heanor on 3 June 1957, just in time for the examination season.

'Billy' (or 'Bunsen') Betts, the last remaining member of teaching staff who had worked under Mr Stoddard, had already announced his retirement at the end of the summer term that year. A chemistry master, he had been at the School for 37 years, the last 12 as Deputy Head.

As we will see over the coming pages, the new Headmaster can certainly be regarded as a moderniser. One of his first actions on arriving at the school was to integrate the sexes more. Classes were, for the most part, already mixed, but Mr Stone removed the rules regarding separate entrances, staircases and playgrounds for boys and girls. He also removed the uniform requirement of caps for boys and berets for girls. At the same time, the uniform was altered so that parents did not have to make a trip to specialist uniform suppliers, Dixon and Parker's, in Nottingham.

Other early decisions had to be made regarding the appointment of a new Deputy Head, now that Mr Betts was leaving. At the July meeting of the governors, the post was awarded to Miss Vera Pugsley, the first time that a mistress had held the position. Howard Houldsworth was now promoted to the post of senior master.

As far as the Local Education Authority's plans were concerned, the growth of the School, in terms of pupil numbers, was completed by 1957, as the last of the two-form entry years took their O-levels. There were now 540 pupils, which included 64 in the sixth form. Space at the School was at a premium, and after years of trying, there was finally movement on the council yard, which was purchased in 1958.

The School's kitchens at this time were rather inadequate. Situated in the wing adjacent to Wilmot Street, the dining room was on the floor above, and all the food had to be hauled up by means of a hand-operated lift. A national scheme to improve school meal facilities made funds available to schools planning major projects which incorporated better school meal provision. Heanor

Grammar School rapidly developed a large-scale plan of extensions into the newly owned part of the site in order to take full advantage of the scheme.

By the time of the publication of the 1959 edition of The Heanorian, all the buildings in the council yard had been demolished. The Headmaster wrote an account of the plans, accompanied by a diagram drawn by the technical drawing master, Mr Diggle, of the three phases of extensions planned. This report is reproduced in full, as it is a clear account which will be recognised by those who knew the School before or after the alterations.

> *The first phase involves the provision of a new three-storey Science Block and the adaptation of rooms in the main building to new purposes. The Science Block will face the Parish Church and will have a 30-foot wide lawn between it and the road. It will provide on the ground floor the senior Chemistry Laboratory with separate Balance Room, Preparation Room and Storeroom, and both boys' and girls' cloakrooms. On the first floor will be a second Chemistry Laboratory and the Biology Laboratory, separated by a Prep. room and a Storeroom. On the second floor will be the senior and second Physics Laboratories with Prep room and Storeroom. There will be staircases at both ends of the building, which will be made to harmonise as far as possible with the church opposite.*
>
> *Also as part of the first phase, the old Chemistry Laboratory is to become the new Library, the Physics Laboratory is to be turned into the new Geography Room, the present Library is to be the new Masters' Room, and the existing Masters' Room will be the new Girls' Rest Room and Medical Inspection Room. The present Headmaster's room will become the School Office and the Head will have a new study in part of Room 3 next door.*
>
> *The boilers have been removed from the old boiler-house and are being replaced by new automatic boilers situated in what was the boy's cycle shed. A new flue for these is being built up through the Head's room and the Physics Laboratory. A new entrance has to be provided for the Woodwork Room. Fire escapes are being provided outside the Dining Room and Rooms 9 and 15.*

DEVELOPMENT PLAN GROUND FLOOR

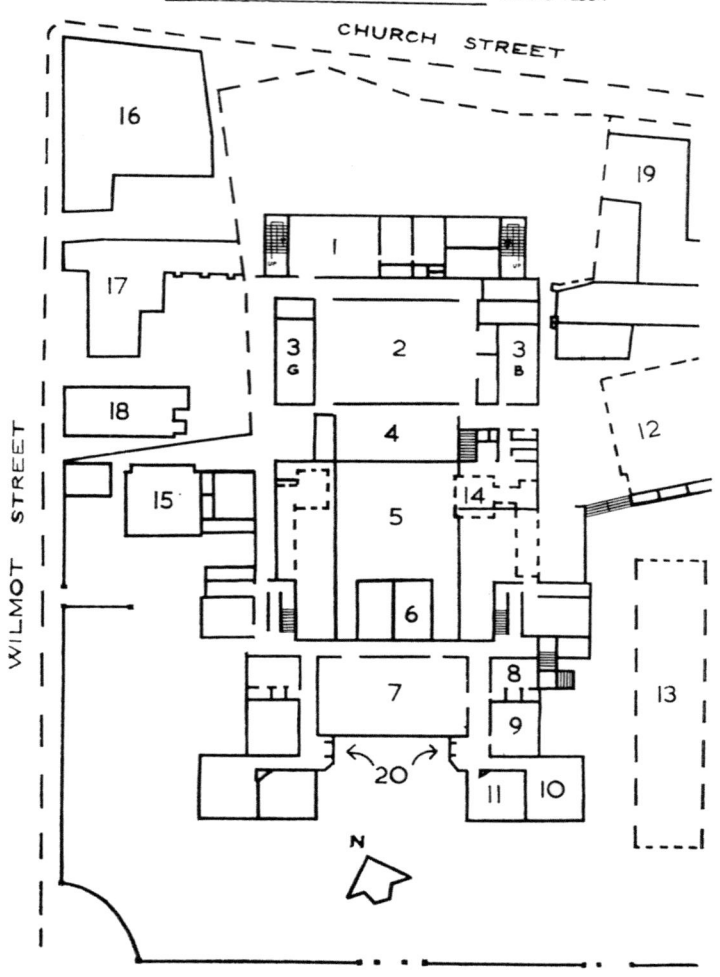

KEY TO DEVELOPMENT PLAN

1. New laboratories, etc.
2. Gymnasium.
3. (B. & G.) Changing Rooms.
   (boys and girls).
4. Stage and Music Room.
5. Assembly Hall.
6. Medical Inspection Room.
7. Hall—converted to library.
8. Secretary's Room.
9. Headmaster's Room.
10. Masters' Staff Room.
11. Senior Mistress's Room and Stationery Store.
12. ⎱ Temporary buildings ultimately
13. ⎰ to be removed.
14. Kitchen.
15. Housecraft Room
    —to be extended.
16. C.W.S. Shops.
17. Public Lavatories.
18. Fire Station.
19. Club.
20. New Main Entrance.

Broken lines indicate walls to be removed, and boundary

In the second phase, which we hope will follow closely on the first, a new Assembly Hall and Kitchen are to be provided, immediately behind the present staff rooms. This Hall will serve also as the Dining Room and the fully equipped stage will also serve as Music Room, with an appropriate store adjacent. At this stage, the present Hall will become a temporary gymnasium.

Finally, in the third stage (and we have no idea when this will be), the space between the Assembly Hall and the Science Block will be filled in with a new gymnasium and changing rooms. Over the boys' changing rooms will be two more storeys, each of three classrooms. Only at this juncture will it be possible at last to do away with the pre-fab buildings. Block A, the old 'tin tab', has already been a 'temporary pre-fab' for nearly 40 years! [sic]

With the provision of a new gymnasium, the present Assembly Hall will become the permanent Library and several other rooms will be used for new purposes.

Speech day in the old hall, around 1960.

Staff photograph 1961: Back row: D.W. Everett, L.T. Winsor, E.H. Jerome, W. Savage, Dr W.L. Liebeschuetz, R. Lindley, W.N. Coxall, D.A. Smedley, D. McNeill, D.G. Todd.
Centre row: Miss E.M. Loveley, Miss R.J. Collens, Miss M.A. Smith, G.P. Gollin, G.R. Dickie, C. Ryde, M.V. Nilsen, Miss G.M. Swindell, Mrs E. Brookes, Miss P.A. Jackson.
Front row: J. Diggle, D.J. Wilkins, W.H. Johnson, A.H. Lawley, H.F. Houldsworth, G.R. Stone, Miss V. Pugsley, S. Bailey, K. Smith, F.V. Mills, Miss M.L. Winfield.

Work progressed well on the first phase of the extension, the main contractors being a local firm, Gee, Walker and Slater, and the science block came into full operation at Easter 1960. Mr Stone would later recall that the heating never worked properly in the science block, as the pipes had to run under the playground from the main school, and that the electronic school bell never reached the building either, causing science lessons to regularly overrun. But these were minor issues. The School now had a 'state of the art' science teaching facility, to replace the science laboratories which had themselves been 'state of the art' in the 1912 building.

The new science block, taken from St. Lawrence's church entrance.

Interior shot of the new biology laboratory.

The second phase of the building work followed closely behind, and in his address to the speech day audience in the spring of 1961, Mr Stone announced that this would be the last such gathering in the old hall. The School was rewired during the summer of 1961, and the new assembly hall and kitchens were taken into use in September that year. The first performance on the new School stage was an adaptation of Molière's *Le Malade Imaginaire* by the School's dramatic society in February 1962. The big worry at the time was the impact on the flooring of the new hall caused by stiletto heels and nails in boys' shoes. At the same time, the old hall was equipped as a 'temporary' gym (with the Caley Robinson mural protected by reinforced glass), and two new classrooms were taken into use over the converted domestic science room.

Whilst these major changes were ongoing, work had not stopped on other issues. A joint effort between the School, the P.T.A. and the Old Students' Association to raise an Eric Sykes Memorial Fund was launched in 1957, with the aim of purchasing an electronic organ. The funds were raised by the autumn term of 1958, and the Miller Martinette Organ was first used at the carol concert at the end of that year. Even before the money had been raised, the next venture had been decided upon. The sports pavilion was struggling (its use had been banned for a short while in 1957, following an accident due to the poor state of the floors). The next fund-raising activity was for a new pavilion for the boys, with the girls using the old one, though this plan would change. By 1962, it had been agreed to enlarge and improve the existing pavilion, for both sexes, and plans were approved in May that year. Although a grant of £2000 was received from the County Council, considerable additional funds (a total of £5265) were required, and the 1963 edition of The Heanorian listed various events held to raise money prior to the work commencing in the summer of that year.

The new pavilion extensions comprised a new frontage with a glass veranda entrance; the changing rooms were equipped with hot and cold showers, and modern toilet facilities. At the formal opening, in May 1964, a charity football match took place between a Heanor Town XI, which included several professionals as well as regular Town players, and Derby County FC, on the school playing fields. The pavilion itself was opened by the chairman of Derby County, Mr Harry Payne. Derby County won the match 5 – 0!

With the pavilion bought and paid for, the P.T.A., true to form, continued fund-raising, their next large purchase being a minibus in 1969.

The extensions to the sports pavilion.

The 1960 edition of The Heanorian listed a few personnel issues to be noted. Mr Colin B. Wood, former Headmaster of Codnor Central Council School, who had taken over as chairman of the governors following the death of Mr Horsley in 1953, was awarded an MBE in June 1959, but died shortly afterwards. He was replaced by Alderman L. Shipley. Another MBE went to Miss E.H. Webb in 1960, for *'public services and services to education in South Derbyshire'*. Miss Webb had been retired for 12 years, but was now one of the governors of the School. At the end of the 1959/60 academic year, Mr Gerald I. ('Wally') Walters, who had been head of history for the last 18 years, left the School. Other significant staff changes during the early 1960s saw the arrival of Mr Colin Wolstenholme, as head of physics, and Mr Don McNeill, as R.E. teacher, in 1961. Miss Pugsley, the Deputy Head, left the School in June 1962, and Miss Olive M. Hyndman took her place as senior mistress and head of French at the start of 1963; Mr Houldsworth was then appointed as Deputy Head. In March 1963, Miss Sheila Randall, a former pupil, was appointed as clerical assistant, and became the school secretary in December 1964, following the departure of Mrs Brookes due to ill-health. These two ladies played a crucial role in the day-to-day running of the School from 1945 to 1976, and Sheila Randall is still actively involved in School issues thirty years after it closed. An old face was seen again at the School at the 1963 speech day, when Mr Allan, who had left 29 years earlier, visited; he was now an MBE, and held the position of Secretary of the Head Masters' Association.

The School continued to show innovation throughout this period under Mr Stone's leadership. In 1960, for example, in conjunction with the Youth Employment Service, the School hosted a careers convention, the first school in southern Derbyshire to do so. The 1960/61 academic year saw a trial with O-levels being taken by a few fourth form pupils, who were clearly destined for university, so that they could spend three years in the sixth form. At the same time, the sixth form timetable was being broadened to allow more general studies, to try to develop pupils' understanding of issues outside their own specialisations. By that time, the School was offering 19 different subjects at A-level, and 21 at O-level. Of particular note was the School's teaching of Russian, something which attracted the attention of the national media; in 1962, Heanor Grammar School was responsible for 12½ per cent of all the Joint Matriculation Board's Russian A-level candidates.

A different sort of success, but again indicating the changing character of the School, was achieved by its tiddleywinks team, inspired by the maths teacher, Mr G.H. Davey, which played various other school and university teams in the early 1960s. Other notable clubs at this time were the school debating society and the cross-country team, both of which won county-wide competitions.

In the autumn of 1963, the School was subject to another (indeed, its last) formal HMI inspection. Needless to say, the improvement in the building stock came in for much praise, though the inspectors commented that Phase 3, which would include the gymnasium, was at least seven years away. There was also criticism of the *'serious lack of hard play area'*, which, had Phase 3 gone ahead, would have only worsened. That said, the enlarged pavilion, which was then almost complete, would improve facilities, and they noted that the School intended to hire the municipal tennis courts, currently under construction next to the memorial park. On the academic side, it was noted that over 10 per cent of pupils had gone on to university over the previous five years. Overall, their impression was of a School *'well aware of the difficulties which must be faced, but in good heart and very well led'*. This was, without a doubt, to be credited to the Headmaster.

A post-extensions aerial view. The new science block and assembly hall are shown, as are Blocks A and B.

The inspectors' comment about '*the difficulties which must be faced*' relates to a wide-scale reorganisation of secondary education in Derbyshire. The future of the grammar school system had been under discussion at national and county level for a number of years. The government were not to push formally towards a full comprehensive school system until 1965, but Derbyshire County Council pre-empted this decision.

This book is not the appropriate forum to discuss the strengths and weaknesses of comprehensive education. There are those who believe, and always did believe, that selection for an academic education was intrinsically unfair, and especially when carried out at the age of 11. Those who supported this view regarded grammar school education as elitist and divisive. On the opposite side, there are others who believe that no amount of creating equal opportunities will ever work, as individual children do not have the same abilities and aptitudes. Their belief is that schools should be able to cater for the differing needs of different children.

The decision was made in early 1963 that all grammar schools were to be abolished in the county and made comprehensive, and that Heanor was to feature in the first wave of this reorganisation. The final eleven-plus exams were held in 1963 for the intake that year.

That Heanor would be one of the first to make the change is not that surprising. The town already had one large secondary modern school at Aldercar, with another one due to open the following year at Heanor Gate. Prior to the introduction of secondary moderns, together with the raising of the school leaving age in 1947, pupils wanting to pass the School Certificate, and subsequently the GCE O-levels, had no choice but to attend the Grammar School. Most would come to the school at 11, but the facility existed, and was used, for pupils to transfer straight into the second, third or fourth forms. With the introduction of the secondary moderns, which themselves offered GCEs, albeit to small numbers, fewer late transfers were now taking place prior to the sixth form. Pupils obtaining O-levels at Aldercar or one of the other secondary schools in the area were able to transfer straight into the sixth form at Heanor Grammar School, and a number did so with notable success.

With the strategic decision to become totally comprehensive, the options were now open for discussion between the heads of the schools involved, alongside the Deputy Director of Education for the County, Chris Phillips. Geoffrey

Stone, Tom Cook, from Aldercar, and Ivor Astley, who was Head of the embryonic Heanor Gate School, held numerous meetings in order to resolve the best way forward within the bounds set by the County, which mainly concerned finance.

The four principal options, as recalled by Mr Stone, were:

1. That Aldercar and Heanor Gate should each become a stand-alone comprehensive school, and that the Grammar School should close, with its staff distributed to the other two. (This had some attraction for the Aldercar Headmaster, who doubtless saw the benefits to his school of increased pupils numbers, especially in view of the fact that a further raising of the school leaving age was now under discussion, following the Newsome Report of 1963. However, this was really not viable in view of the large amount of money spent on Heanor Grammar School over the previous few years.)

2. That Heanor Gate become a stand-alone comprehensive school, with Aldercar and Heanor Grammar School forming another on split sites, and with Aldercar being the lower school. (This would have caused major logistical problems in view of their locations, and was unacceptable to Mr Stone and Mr Cook alike.)

3. That Heanor Gate and Aldercar both become 11 – 16 comprehensives, with the Grammar School as a sixth form centre. (Whilst this had some major attractions, again the recent expensive extensions to Heanor Grammar School, giving it a capacity for some 540 pupils, would have meant that its facilities would be grossly underused; economically, this option was not viable at that time.)

4. That Heanor Gate and Aldercar be 11 – 16 schools, but with a partial transfer at the age of 13 or 14 to the Grammar School, which would also operate the sixth form for the area. This system was known as the *'Leicestershire model'*. (The benefit of this was that the numbers transferring each year could be made to match the accommodation available in each of the schools. Another advantage, or disadvantage, depending on one's viewpoint, was that there was still an element of selection, though at a later age, and not by exam, and under another name.)

The Leicestershire Model was the chosen option.

However, the decision still had to be made regarding the age at which the transfers from Aldercar and Heanor Gate were to take place, and what criteria were to be used. The initial decision was that children could move schools at the age of 13+ (i.e. into the third form), on what was called *'guided parental option'*. What this meant, was that Aldercar and Heanor Gate Schools advised parents on whether or not their children should move to the Grammar School, but that parents did not have to follow that advice. This was followed by a second option to transfer a year later, straight into the fourth form, but this was to be by *'parental option'* alone. The existing option to transfer into the sixth form after GCEs or CSEs (the Certificate of Secondary Education was introduced in the 1964/5 academic year) remained unchanged.

And so the School had survived, for now, the abolition of grammar school status. Although it was planned that pupil numbers would not fall dramatically, it was equally clear that there would be no further major building programmes; effectively Phase 3 was abandoned. From this point, the County Council referred to the School as 'Heanor Secondary School'. But the School itself made no attempt to alter its name; as far as its pupils and the general public were concerned, it was still Heanor Grammar School!

Chapter 10

The Leicestershire Model, 1964 - 1973

For anybody not involved in the actual organisation, the first few years of the use of the Leicestershire model at Heanor appear to have been extremely confusing. Indeed, even Mr Stone, one of the parties to the decision (albeit not a willing one), called the resulting system *'a cumbersome nonsense that could not last'*.

The start of the 1964/5 year saw, for the first time since 1893, no 11-year-old pupils at Heanor Grammar School, as all went to Aldercar or Heanor Gate. The first form was no more! At the speech day in March 1965, Mr Stone pointed out one side effect of this change, namely that the previous year's first formers were destined to be the youngest members of the school for three consecutive years. However, to keep the numbers up, 60 pupils transferred from Aldercar straight into the fourth and fifth forms to work on GCE courses. The Head expressed his concerns, in private, that moving the children so late in their school life was giving them totally inadequate time to prepare for their GCEs. Indeed, out of the first intake of 24 pupils directly into the fifth form, only 44 GCE O-level passes (along with a substantial number of CSEs) were obtained in 1965. However, when it is remembered that they had only been doing the course for one academic year, their achievement was not insignificant. After a meeting with the parents of pupils who had moved from Aldercar into the fourth form, between 10 and 15 later withdrew their children from the School; some stated that they had believed that the transfer had been compulsory. Clearly the communication of the reorganisation could have been improved.

With the decision having been taken that the School would not be closing following the move to quasi-comprehensive status, the Education Authority were still able to spend money on it. In 1964, the Grammar School became one of only three schools in the county to be equipped with a language laboratory, consisting of 32 booths where pupils could work on their speaking and listening skills. Further work saw the conversion of B Block, the HORSA building, into a boys' practical block, with rooms for woodwork, metalwork and engineering drawing classes.

The change in the make-up of the School, and the development of society generally in the 1960s, were reflected by changes to the school magazine. Still called The Heanorian, it now lost its traditional look, along with the school badge on the front cover. Each subsequent edition of the magazine had a different cover design. The paper size was also increased, and the content remained similar, but with an increased use of photographs (though school team photos were now seldom printed).

A change of style: The Heanorian magazine, 1965 – 1969.

The autumn of 1965 saw the publication of Circular 10/65 by the Department of Education, under the Minister, Anthony Crosland. Effectively, the circular confirmed the decision made by Derbyshire two years earlier, and the document commenced with the clear statement that, *'It is the Government's declared objective to end selection at eleven plus and to eliminate separatism in secondary education.'* All education committees were *'requested'* to convert their schools to the comprehensive system. This request was backed up by ensuring that government funding would only go to those authorities who complied. Immediately, the governors at Heanor were discussing its impact on the School, and whether further reorganisation was already necessary. The possibility of the School becoming a sixth form college, but with an extended catchment area, was again discussed. Although the circular does not feature in the minutes again, it should not be forgotten.

The School from Mundy Street, 1966.

The 1965/6 year saw a much reduced intake of pupils, including the first to transfer from Heanor Gate; the total number of children at the Grammar School was now 380, having fallen from its peak of 550. However, this was all part of the plan, and student numbers were planned to rise considerably again over the next few years. The 1966 intake saw 94 pupils transferring to the third and fourth forms, with 129 in 1967, and 160 in 1968, of whom 117 were third formers. This was the largest third form in the School's history, only surpassed in the final two years of the School when 120 pupils were admitted each year.

However, the problems of pupils transferring at different stages, which had been recognised at the outset, still remained. After further discussions it was decided that the system needed to be simplified, and that from 1969 the transfer, still by *'guided parental option'*, would only take place at the age of

13. This would give pupils three full academic years before their O-levels, and, Mr Stone argues, *'no pupil lost out on opportunities through the existence of the choice at 13+'*, as both the 'feeder' schools had well established GCE groups of their own by this time. The transfer into the sixth form continued as before, with a steady flow of pupils.

The period after the 1964 re-organisation saw major changes in the style and management of the School. We have already seen how the Headmaster started changing some school traditions as soon as he arrived. These changes would now gather pace. This cannot be put down solely to the changes in society in the 1960s – the developments at Heanor Grammar School, whilst not in themselves unique, were truly innovative. And whilst a move towards 'child-centred' education was occurring across the country, the rate of change at Heanor was particularly noticeable. There is no doubt that some of the community would have been unhappy with the general liberalisation of the regime.

Part of the reason for change was, undoubtedly, due to the changing structure of the School. It is also clear that the liberalisation was not something which just happened – it was clearly planned. The Headmaster himself talked about this at the 1966 speech day:

> *We now have few pupils under 14 years of age and the whole atmosphere of the school is consequently changing. We are gradually, but steadily making rules and courses less rigid, leaving more to the choice and good sense of the pupils.*

One of the changes made in that year was the abolition of the house system which had first been set up in 1913. The house trophy, which was normally awarded to Ray, Flamstead or Howitt, is engraved with the winners for 1966: *'Team "E", Form G'*. The removal of the house system was, to a point, understandable; pupils were coming into the school much later, and some would only be there for a couple of years. This left little time for the pupils to develop a sense of belonging to another tier of the system. But for old students, who still looked back fondly to their membership of a school house, this must have been a bitter blow.

The 1967 speech day had more comments from Mr Stone on liberalisation:

> *We now have no formal punishment system; we have no school prefects...; we have liberalised our approach to school uniform a lot..., and we now have an active School Advisory Council.*

He went on to tell the audience that the sixth form now had well over 100 pupils – it is doubtless not a coincidence that the sixth form numbers rose so significantly (more than 50 per cent in three years) at the same time as the regime was being relaxed.

Heanor Grammar School was one of only a few schools in the country to have a school council, and this attracted the attention of the national media. An item in the Guardian in 1968 described the workings of the school council at Heanor:

> *To encourage as many as possible to transfer to it from the feeder schools, it was decided to try to create a more adult environment...*
>
> *It has been made clear by the head that he is not able to act on all motions before the council. But where he cannot act, he gives a reasoned explanation why. Similarly, he has undertaken to answer all questions fully...*
>
> *Pupils feel that they know why things happen, and that they can question and influence policy. The staff has found that the pupils have shown themselves to be 'responsible', with many constructive suggestions, as well as criticisms and questions.*

As well as the school council, with 30 pupil-members and chaired by the Headmaster, there was also a separate sixth form committee. This had an elected chairman and vice-chairman, who were the equivalent of the former head boy and head girl. The school council had sub-committees to deal with finance (it ran its own 'tuckshop'), and uniform.

Whilst the Headmaster, as shown from the article, still retained overall control, the school council did take an active part in the development of the School. For example, one decision of the council was actually to reverse a previous policy change, and reintroduce the house system. The three previous houses were brought back in 1969, and were now joined by a fourth house, Mundy.

The reintroduction of houses saw a growth, again, in the amount of sporting competition in the School. Sports day had been discontinued along with the houses, but now returned in 1970, albeit on a much scaled-down format. The school magazine reported that no records were broken that year, *'as all races were judged in metres for the first time'*. The following year, The Heanorian reported the no doubt welcome news that the School had started using the *'new William Gregg V.C. Baths in Heanor'*. (It is of note that the governors had been informed of the District Council's consideration to build a new *'public baths and gym'* as early as 1938.) At last, there was to be no more freezing at Langley! The revived sports day was short-lived, however, for in 1972, although the date was published in the school calendar, the magazine tells of *'the lack of interest that led to the cancelling of Sports Day'*.

By 1966, the sixth form had their own room, but in the following year the 'Tin Tab' had been given over to them, and was now named the 'sixth form centre'. The building was equipped with a lounge, private study room and three sixth form classrooms. The lounge had fitted carpets, easy chairs and a television. There was some difference between the upper and lower sixth, as the younger pupils had to do private study in a workroom, whereas the older ones could use the lounge.

The sixth form committee set their own uniform, but, again, within the limits set out by the Headmaster; so, interestingly, the regulation tie and blazer were still retained. The committee enabled a two-way flow of information, and was sometimes used by the School to pass on instructions, rather than being given by the staff themselves. An example of this was minuted in 1969: *'Mr Stone has asked that the Committee should do something to prevent the amorous behaviour which is occurring in the lounge. Will all people concerned please take note!'* Not the sort of instruction that Mr Stoddard would have had to give!

Perhaps the biggest break with tradition was announced at speech day in the spring of 1969, namely that this was to be the last such event. The school magazine later in the year added that the removal of speech day was also accompanied by the removal of *'prizes'* for achievement. These had been given annually for many years, usually donated by individual old students, or by the Old Students' Association. The author of the 'School News' section of the magazine stated: *'Books as prizes for academic achievement may have outlived their usefulness.'*

At the final speech day, mention was also made of a history of the School which was nearing completion, being written by Mrs Pam Carter, assisted by Rex Calladine. This publication never went ahead, even though the Head was already able to inform the audience how much it would cost (7/6d). A rough draft of the work, which was based primarily on the contents of the school magazines over the years, still exists.

Despite the liberal standards at Heanor Grammar School, life at the school was certainly not a 'free-for-all', and discipline was maintained. For example, in 1973 a sixth form boy was threatened with expulsion if he did not get his hair cut – the boy gave in! During the same year, Mr Stone reported twice to the governors his concerns regarding the National Union of School Students, who *'had caused some unrest in the School, but direct confrontation was being avoided'*. Heanor pupils had a freer life than many of their counterparts, but obviously not all were satisfied with this.

Staffing changes during the late 1960s and early 1970s did not involve many long-service members, as most of them had already left. New arrivals, although they may not yet know it, were not to stay at the School throughout their careers. One arrival who should be mentioned though was the new chairman of the governors in 1967, Leslie Lloyd, a former pupil who was now director at Aristoc in Langley Mill. The 1965 Heanorian reported the deaths of two former Headmasters during the previous year, Mr Allan and Mr Spencer. In 1966, the magazine printed an obituary for Miss Pugsley. In 1970, the magazine reported the death of former pupil and later school secretary, Mrs M.J.E. Brookes, and in 1971, an obituary was printed for Mr 'Joey' Hancock, who had taught at the School from 1920 to 1956. The only notable retirement of this period was that of Miss Margaret L. ('Winnie') Winfield, in 1970, who had been at the School, as English teacher, since 1932; Miss Winfield would actually return for a short period in 1973. On the domestic front, Miss M. Smith retired in 1966; she had worked in the school kitchen for 20 years, including eight as senior cook. The same year, the head caretaker for the last 11 years, Mr Fred Orme, also retired.

The late 1960s saw fewer changes than previously to the structure of the building. We have already seen how, yet again, Block A, the 'Tin Tab', was adapted to meet the changing requirements of the School. Another change was in the science block. Within a short time of the block's opening, the use of a large portion of the ground floor as cloakrooms was seen as a waste of space.

Initial plans were to turn this into a further laboratory, but this proved unfeasible. By 1968, however, the cloakrooms had been replaced by a tiered lecture room, with visual aid facilities and seating for up to 60 pupils. Another, perhaps not very noticeable change, related to a wartime relic on the playing fields. As early as 1946, the governors had recommended that the air raid shelters should be removed, but nothing was done. By 1966, they were in an insanitary condition, and the governors again were asking for their demolition. This still did not happen, but three years later the entrances and the top of the shelters were finally concreted over to prevent access.

With no likelihood of Phase 3 of the extensions happening, there was still some movement, albeit small, towards providing more accommodation. When the School had acquired the council yard in the 1950s, this left little of the 'island' (bordered by Church Street, Ilkeston Road, Mundy Street and Wilmot Street) which did not belong to the School. Some of what remained was the Co-op Store, which was clearly not accessible.

However, as had been tried earlier, the Head still had his eyes on the old fire station on Wilmot Street, for use as a Music Centre. Before the extensions, music had been based in the old dining room for lessons and practice. After the new hall was built, the stage served a dual role as a music room. Whilst an improvement, this was still was not very satisfactory: the only sound-proofing was the stage curtain, and once a stage production was being planned, the area was unusable for other purposes.

The fire station had been built in 1923, but had long since lost its original purpose, and was now only used by the Heanor Urban District Council for storage. When initial discussions took place, in 1965, the Council refused to sell the building, but two years later they agreed to lease it to the County Council for use by the School. Nothing in life is simple though, and it was not until March 1971 that the keys were finally handed over. The building was little more than a shell, and needed a lot of work doing on it. Mr Stone's comments at the time were that he '*hoped the money would be handed over to make it usable before Mr Walter Savage retired*'.

At the March 1968 governors' meeting, it was commented that the '*change in character*' of the School, with later entry, meant that more time and concentration were required for academic work. This had had a knock-on effect, and many societies, even the orchestra, might go by the board.

However, the development of music in the curriculum itself continued with vigour, hence the pressure to acquire the fire station. Although the new music studio was not large, it was a great improvement, especially since it was separate from the main building. The School acquired a wide range of instruments (including a variety of brass instruments from a Marines' band which had disbanded), and a number of peripatetic teachers visited to give individual tuition both during and after school hours. In the following few years, the School was chosen as the venue for the South Derbyshire Music School, which operated on Saturdays, with participants from all over the region.

Whilst it is true that the number of societies and extra-curricular groups mentioned in The Heanorian diminished during this period, there were exceptions. The best example of this was the run of productions of Gilbert and Sullivan operettas between 1963 and 1972. These were started by Mr David Wilkins, the head of history, who acted as producer, and continued after he left by the senior mistress, Miss Olive Hyndman. The first production, *Patience*, was given in the new hall instead of a school play that year, in conjunction with the dramatic society. In 1965, a production of *Iolanthe* was given, and under the guidance of Walter Savage, a Gilbert and Sullivan operetta became an annual event: *Trial by Jury* (1966), *The Mikado* (1967), *The Gondoliers* (1968), *The Yeoman of the Guard* (1969), *Patience* (1970), *The Pirates of Penzance* (1971), and *The Mikado* (1972). In 1973, there was a return to drama (though there had been a number of one-act compilations during the late 1960s), but still with a musical theme, with *Oh What a Lovely War*.

After the hiccup of the 1964 reorganisation, academically the School was going from strength to strength. The 1968 examination results were the best ever seen by the School – the pupils doing O-levels that year were the last of the eleven plus intake of 1963, together with later-entry pupils from other years. There were 113 pupils in the year, and 69 passed in five or more subjects. In the A-level year, 37 students obtained two or more passes. That year no less that 41 students went on to some type of higher education. A fitting way to hold a final speech day!

Photographs from the 1970 production of Gilbert and Sullivan's *Patience*.

As already mentioned, the number of students in the sixth form was rising. In 1971, 24 per cent of pupils stayed on after taking their O-levels, a rise of 7 per cent in four years. The school leaving age rose to 16 years in September 1972, and the indications were that this would prompt even more pupils to stay at school into the sixth form.

The Leicestershire Model had left Heanor with an element of selection, which had been contrary to the initial intentions of the County Council. The first action of the Department of Education following the election of a Conservative Government in 1970 (under Education Minister Margaret Thatcher) was to abandon Circular 10/65. However, the replacement circular left issues regarding the conversion to comprehensive education firmly with the local authorities. Derbyshire, as many other counties, had made its decision, and still intended to achieve a totally comprehensive system. In fact, nationally, more schools became comprehensive under Margaret Thatcher than under her Labour predecessors. With steadily rising numbers of students staying on for A-levels, and well established secondary schools capable of holding higher numbers, the time had been reached for the reorganisation in Heanor to be completed.

A photograph from 1971 showing the 'Tin Tab' from Ilkeston Road.

Chapter 11

The Final Reorganisation, 1973 - 1976

The reorganisation of secondary education in the area had never been finished; the steps in 1964 had always been regarded by those involved as a preliminary first stage to a further major change, even though this was not made public at the time. By 1971, the County believed that the time had come to advance the comprehensive system, and there was general concern about how the Leicestershire Model at Heanor was working. In addition, the number of pupils was falling again – in 1971/2 there were 419 pupils at the Grammar School, down nearly 60 in four years, and of these 108 were in the sixth form. In 1971, because of the reduction in the number of sixth formers, The Heanorian reported,

> *declining numbers in the sixth form no longer warranted the exclusive use by the sixth of the whole block* [Block A], *and so it had been decided to put the four classrooms there to the further use of the whole school. Sixth upper only would use the lounge, and room thirteen in the main block would be the private study room and sixth lower's common room.*

A preferred option for some was the creation of a sixth form college based on the Heanor Grammar School site. However, with the number of students staying on for A-levels, this option was still not viable unless the catchment area was considerably increased. In March 1972, the governors came up with a number of options, some of which have already been mentioned:

1. The three secondary schools could be merged and run as a single school on three sites. This would create major logistical problems, and was not really given any serious consideration.

2. Heanor Gate could merge with the Grammar School, as an 11 – 18 school. The two schools were within relatively easy walking distance, so this might have been feasible. Aldercar would remain 11 – 16, with pupils transferring to Heanor after O-levels. The problem with this option would be that Aldercar could be seen as a 'poor relation', and as such the option would possibly not be acceptable to part of the community.

3. Similar to the initial idea of a sixth form college, the Grammar School could merge with the South East Derbyshire College of Further Education to form a 'junior college,' catering for all aspects of post-16 education.

A further special meeting of the governors was held in April, and it was agreed to push ahead with the junior college proposal.

Although this was the terminology used, what was actually being proposed, and what subsequently emerged, was not a 'junior college' (an early name for a 'sixth form college'), but rather a 'tertiary college'. The main difference between a tertiary college and a sixth form college is that the former offers education and training for all students over the compulsory school leaving age, with no maximum age limit, whereas the latter only deals with students between the ages of 16 and 19 years. Likewise, a tertiary college is different from a college of further education, which tends to operate in co-existence with other schools and colleges, offering specific subjects only. The planned college at Heanor would operate under further education rules, but would be the sole provider of education for students over 16 in the area.

Again, whilst Heanor was not the first to go down this route, it was nevertheless an early player. The first tertiary college had been established in 1970, in Exeter, followed shortly afterwards by others in Yeovil, Bridgewater, Nelson and Colne, and Andover. In the latter two cases, the colleges had been formed by amalgamating a Grammar School with a Technical College.

One possible problem with the proposal was that the South East Derbyshire College of Further Education had itself only recently been formed by the merger of the Heanor Technical College with the Ilkeston College of Further Education. As we have already seen, Heanor Technical College had developed in the 1930s, and offered a number of technical and engineering subjects, along with secretarial and business courses. Ilkeston College was a post-war development which, during the 1960s, added an academic studies department to offer O- and A-levels to mature students.

There were already regular links between the existing college and the Grammar School. The main example of this was the music centre in the fire station, which had been a joint project, but equally students from either establishment could be allocated a course at the other, where appropriate.

When the Heanor and Ilkeston colleges had merged, the principal of the Ilkeston College had retired; the new Principal was Tony Harmer, a civil engineer who had been in charge of Heanor College. One issue which would have to be resolved was the question of leadership of the new institution. In the end, this was determined by Mr Stone agreeing to become the Associate Principal of the new establishment; he was to have responsibility for the academic organisation of the College, while Mr Harmer retained responsibility for organisational and administrative issues.

There were other practical problems to resolve, principally due to the difference in staffing arrangements for schools and further education colleges. The Headmaster was adamant, and was successful in ensuring, that none of his existing staff should lose out by transferring to further education rules. He persuaded the Department of Education and the Local Education Authority to agree to this, even though some of the staff did not meet the criteria for their new posts, and even though the new college could not, at least at first, justify all of the newly-created positions, in terms of the number of students involved. Mr Stone argued that that the number of students would rapidly increase in the new college, and he was right.

A unique problem, though, was what was going to happen to the pupils at Heanor Grammar School on the date that the new college was established. The sixth formers presented no problem, but there would still be pupils working for their O-levels, who were too young, legally, to attend a further education college. One option considered was that existing school pupils would, on paper, be transferred to Heanor Gate. However, this would undoubtedly have caused a protest by the parents of those involved, and so a different, and innovative, solution was developed. Heanor Grammar School would continue to exist, as a legal entity, alongside the College, until the last pupil had finished the fifth form. All the staff at Heanor Grammar School would transfer to the College, but would continue to teach Grammar School pupils as well as College students. However, two members of staff, namely Mr Stone and Mr Houldsworth, although paid by the College, would also continue to be the staff of the 'notional' Grammar School. When this was finally put into action, this meant that, de facto, Heanor Grammar School had the worst teacher-pupil ratio in the country, with just two staff to 240 pupils! The County had expected the Department of Education to reject this solution, but they agreed to it with relative ease.

Work on these plans was progressed throughout 1972 and the early part of 1973. At the meeting of the governors in May 1973, they were informed that the last intake of third form pupils would be in September 1973, and that the new College would come into existence in September 1974, at which time the sixth form students would transfer to the College. It was also stated that, in order to cater for the increased number of pupils, Heanor Gate would require additional building work; this would not be completed until 1976, and in the meantime Grammar School accommodation would be utilised.

Having agreed in principle to the plans, the Education Authority considered whether to further extend the proposals to include the schools at Ilkeston. This would have made sense, since the new College would be split between the towns anyway. A series of public meetings was held in both areas. There was opposition to the closure of the Grammar School in Heanor, and the Ripley and Heanor News carried several letters and articles on the subject. However, at least for the parents of existing pupils, criticism of the proposals was moderated by the knowledge that the same staff would still be involved, and that their children would, in most cases, still be taught in the same building. Opposition to the plan in Ilkeston, however, was much greater, and that part of the proposal was scrapped – Ilkeston Grammar School retained its sixth form, but, in the end, still became comprehensive.

The 1972 edition of The Heanorian, published shortly before the proposals for reorganisation were made public, changed in style again. Proudly entitled 'The New Heanorian', it was A4 in size, with numerous photographs of staff members on the cover. It was, perhaps, because of the number of photographs, that comment was made to the governors about the *'high cost of production'*. The next edition (published late) in the last term of 1973/4 was entitled 'The Last Heanorian'. Fittingly, it sported a black cover with a few photographs of parts of the School building. The editors started by complaining about the lack of items submitted for the magazine – strangely reminiscent of many such comments in the 1910s and 1920s!

This final edition reported a number of departures from the school, including two long-serving teachers' retirements, Mr W.H. Johnson (at the school since 1948), and Mr W. Savage, who had retired at Christmas 1972, after 21 years at the school. The next page of the magazine carried an obituary to Walter Savage, who had died in May 1974, just before the magazine's publication. Although he had finished full time teaching in 1972, he continued to give some part-time tuition to sixth formers, and had another Gilbert and Sullivan production in rehearsal at the time of his death.

The last four school magazines, including The New Heanorian (1972), and The Last Heanorian (1974).

It is, perhaps, ironic that the minutes of the final meeting of the governors, in June 1974, prior to the implementation of the plans referred, yet again, to 'Block A'. The minutes stated that the building *'is believed not to be in a very safe condition, but is required for a further two years'*. At the same meeting, a

School Staff, early 1970s. Back row: Jean Turner, Pat Harris, Fred Mills, Don McNeil, Bob Woolley, John Diggle, Ted Jerome, Stuart Dix, Glenys Elliott.
Centre row: Sheila Clayton, Christine Cooke, George Dickie, Colin Wolstenholme, Sid Bailey, Sandra Bruce, Sheila Randall, Vera Smith, Betty Burdett.
Front row: Juliet Pragnell, Joan Williams, Alec Lawley, Olive Hyndman, Geoffrey Stone, Howard Houldsworth, Anne Nixon, Margaret Viles, Margaret Kerr.

letter from the University of Nottingham gave thanks for allowing them to use the School for teaching practice over many years.

And so, at the start of September 1974, the building was now owned by the College. Some commentators regard the summer of 1974 as the closing date of the School (even Mr Stone has used this date on occasions). However, a school is more than just a building. There may have been no fresh intake of school pupils, but there was a fourth and fifth form for whom Heanor Grammar School most definitely still existed. There were also quite a few Heanor Gate pupils on the premises, due to the building work at their own school; but everyone else was a student of the new South East Derbyshire College.

The governors were told, at their meeting that month, that they now had a *'reduced responsibility in relation to the merger'*, and Mr Stone presented his report to them:

> *As from 1 September, the premises which formerly belonged to the School, and all the Staff, except the School Meals staff, became the responsibility of the new South East Derbyshire College.*
>
> *So the School Governors are now only responsible for keeping a 'watching brief' on behalf of the 240 fourth and fifth form pupils, who are all that remain of the school.*

The Head also spelled out the problems over integrating the terms, holidays, and lesson times of the college and the school, which were running side by side. The school day and the school year were fixed, but, as far as was possible, the School and College were brought into line.

Later in the year the 'Tin Tab' had obviously deteriorated further, and the decision was made that it could not continue beyond the summer of 1975. By now the oldest part of the School, it was then finally demolished, 67 years after being temporarily added to Heanor Hall,

At the end of the academic year 1974/5, with just one more year to go, the decision was made to close the school kitchen, leaving the 1975 fifth formers to eat at the College canteen on Ilkeston Road, next to Heanor library. Pupils were assured that they would continue to pay school-meal prices, rather than college prices. It was also decided to relax the uniform rules for the 120 remaining pupils, as it seemed unfair to require them to purchase any major new items of uniform. This same meeting discussed problems being caused by the large number of Heanor Gate pupils on the site. They were also told that the library and geography rooms, the rooms which in 1912 had been set up as the chemistry and physics laboratories, were going to be divided into smaller classrooms.

The 'temporary' building, finally demolished after nearly 70 years!

The final year of the school came and went, with now just 120 pupils and many 'SEDCol' students. The new College, with its mix of academic and non-academic courses was proving popular, and many students transferred from those Ilkeston schools which had previously refused to join the new partnership.

In May 1976, with only weeks to go before the formal closure of the School, a special meeting of the governors took place. Also invited to participate were members of the Parents' Association, the Old Students' Association, staff, and retired staff. The purpose of the meeting was to decide what should happen to items of property which could be argued did not belong to the College or the County Council. The decisions of this meeting are listed below:

The School trophies were to be passed to the two feeder-schools at Heanor Gate and Aldercar.

The Caley Robinson War Memorial was in too fragile a condition to be moved, and should be left in situ.

The War Memorial Chair and Lectern should be put into storage.

A coin collection donated to the School by Mr (later Sir) Albert Martin should be passed to the county museum at Derby. (This decision was subject to more correspondence at County level, after it was discovered that the collection was valued at far more than anyone thought. However, the decision to donate it to the museum stood.)

The portrait of Ralph Stoddard was to be temporarily moved to the Headmaster's office (which was still used by Mr Stone in his capacity as Associate Principal of the College), but thereafter was to be returned to the old hall. A plaque was to be added to the photograph, so that the portrait would always be identifiable.

A letter from George Bernard Shaw sent in response to a letter from a group of pupils in 1947 was to be passed to the county archives. The archivist had also expressed an interest in the general records of the School.

A final meeting of the governors took place on 17 May 1976, and the last ever pupils of Heanor Grammar School attended, compulsorily, on 26 May, though exams continued into June.

Interviewed for the Derby Evening Telegraph, Mr Stone said:

> *It is enormously sad that an institution which has contributed so much to the life of the locality should actually finish. But the tradition remains and the service has been given. We hope that something of what this school stood for in the community can be carried on, in the college and in the schools at Heanor Gate and Aldercar.*

Thirty years on, the legacy of Heanor Grammar School still remains.

Two Headmasters.
The last Head, Geoffrey Stone, in front of the portrait of the first,
Ralph Stoddard.
©Derby Evening Telegraph. Reprinted with permission.

Chapter 12

The Legacy

The School had now closed, and that could be the end of the story. But there are a few items still worthy of note before the history of the School is completed.

Although the School closed, it was not in the way of so many school closures. The building was not demolished, and the staff were not out of work. It must be remembered that the School closed in order to merge with another establishment to create a new entity; Heanor Grammar School was an integral component of South East Derbyshire College.

Although it was considered, this book will not cover the development of the College since 1974. However, there are a few issues which directly concern the Mundy Street site.

As previously stated, all the staff moved to new posts in the College, most of them based in the same building at the Heanor branch. Geoffrey Stone, now the Associate Principal, stayed on until his retirement at Easter 1979.

In the thirty years of its existence, the South East Derbyshire College has gone through stages of both expansion and contraction, and it is likely that this will continue in the future, especially since it has been a self-funding body since 1993.

During the mid 1990s, there were discussions about the future of the Mundy Street site (as indeed there still are). A college document at the start of 1997 informed the staff that it had been decided to keep the site and to designate it as a '*core building*'. One of the major factors behind this decision was the fact that the original school is a Grade II listed building, making it so much harder to sell. This decision meant that the College were now to improve the building, with new facilities. As part of the changes, Block B, the old HORSA unit, would finally be demolished, after giving almost 50 years 'temporary' service. The Mundy Street hall (the 'new' one from 1961) was to become a learning resource centre with library and IT facilities. It is still in use as such today, though the basic layout of the hall, with its stage and blocked-up servery to where the kitchen was, is still very recognisable. Another part of the project included the restoration to a light oak colour of the wood panelling in the corridors of the old School; the panelling is still in excellent condition today.

The corridor adjacent to the old hall, 2008. The wood panelling still in excellent condition.

After the work was completed, the site was relaunched in October 1997. Interestingly, at that time, the College called it 'The Old Heanor Grammar School Centre', a name which has now been dropped. The centre was formally opened by Arlene McCarthy, M.E.P. for the Peak District, and a plaque in the old hall commemorates this. The site is now called the 'Sixth Form Centre', which is what many of the key players in the 1960s and 1970s had wanted. The difference between the plans then, and the reality now, is that the College is not the sole provider of sixth form education in the Heanor area – Heanor Gate Science College has a thriving sixth form, and a 'Post 16 Centre' is due to open at the Aldercar Community Language College in 2008.

Shortly after the 1997 relaunch of the Mundy Street site, the College acquired another school building in Ilkeston, the former Cavendish School. This was now designated as the Cavendish Arts Centre, specialising in art, music, media and performing arts. The site of the original Ilkeston College of Further Education, on Field Road, at Ilkeston, continues as the College's vocational academy.

The College also owns the former Co-op at the junction of Church Street and Wilmot Street in Heanor. For a period in the early 2000s this was an IT centre, but at the present time the ground floor is no longer in use. The College now has control of more of the 'island' site than ever before. However, the fire station, which was leased to the School and then to the College as a music centre, has been disused for a number of years. Now under the ownership of the Heanor Town Council, the building has been renovated and earmarked for 'arts and heritage' purposes.

One major part of the original College no longer exists, namely the former Heanor Mining College on Ilkeston Road. And, with the loss of that building, the old school playing fields, along with the sports pavilion, have gone. Most of the site has been used for housing, but a section of the playing fields became the site of a new school, the Mundy CE Voluntary Controlled Junior School to replace the Mundy Street School premises. The new school opened in 2005, and has its entrance on Lockton Avenue. It was not until this new school was built that the playing field air-raid shelters were finally removed (despite some local concern that they were of 'historical interest').

Taken from the site of Block B, this 2008 photograph shows 'The Atrium', as well as the science block and the church tower.

The old School today looks, from the outside, rather weary in places, and has, like so many other buildings, suffered its share of vandalism and lack of maintenance. But anyone taking a tour inside the building would be pleasantly surprised at how little has changed. There is a large new reception area, called 'the Atrium', on the side of the 'new hall' facing Ilkeston Road. But the old corridors are still the same as they were in the 1970s. The classrooms still have the original cupboards which were installed because Mr Stoddard did not want a library. The labs in the science block are still equipped with some of their 1960s work benches, though the lecture theatre on the ground floor of the science block is now an additional laboratory. The old hall still has the Caley Robinson memorial for those who fell in the First World War; it still has the Honours Boards listing the former head boys and head girls, in the position where Mr Stoddard wanted to hang the paintings by Bissill.

Education beyond the age of 16 has changed considerably over the last 30 years, and continues to do so. There can be no certainty that South East Derbyshire College, or any other college, will exist in its present form in another 30 years. It is to be hoped that whatever the future of the site, the building itself will be preserved as much as possible. Its listed building status will assist in this, but perhaps of more significance is the strength of the old School's supporters.

On many occasions during this book, the Old Students' Association has been mentioned. They were formed at the earliest stages, and were a constant source of fund-raising over the years, especially, though not exclusively, in relation to the war memorials.

Over the years of the School, the O.S.A. had periods where its activities dwindled through lack of support only to resurface after a few years. The same has happened since the School closed.

Today, there is a very active Old Students' Association, despite it being over 30 years since anyone attended Heanor Grammar School. The Association today is far less formal than in the past; there are no monthly committee meetings and no annual membership fee. But for a school which no longer exists it is surprisingly active.

In the first years after the School's closure, there is little evidence of any structured gatherings of past pupils, although some reunions clearly did occur.

In 1977 an advert in a local newspaper led to a gathering of old students at Heanor Town Hall, and in 1978, the first reunion dinner took place. This was following the precedent, first seen in September 1927, of an O.S.A. annual dinner. (That said, the first annual reunion of the Old Students' Association took place in 1905, just 12 years after the school was founded.) The new reunions became an annual event, albeit initially aimed at students from the 1920s and 1930s. In 1984, the organisation of the events was taken over by Ron and Glenis Clarke, and the decision was made to make the reunions open to all 'Old Heanorians'. Ron and Glenis continued to organise the reunions until 2002, and then continued as presidents of the Association. Reunions now take place twice a year, at Easter and in October. Although they have been held elsewhere, since October 2002 they have taken place in the old hall at the School. At the 1993 reunion, over 200 people attended. As with other schools, there have also been many individual year reunions take place.

In another development, a separate annual reunion commenced in 1998 for past players of the Old Heanorians Football Club, which had flourished for several decades before ceasing in the 1982. The reunion dinner, together with a couple of golfing reunions each year, still takes place.

In October 1988, the Old Students' Association arranged a service of dedication of the war memorial furniture and the book of remembrance at All Saints Church, Marlpool, where the items still remain. After being put into storage in 1976, the chair and lectern were 'lost' in the basement at Mundy Street. After a considerable search, the items were found again and restored by Mr Derek Camm. At the same time, a plaque was placed in the old hall of the school giving their new location.

In 1993, a pamphlet was produced to celebrate the centenary of the founding of the School. This contained an article by Mr Stone, excerpts from Mr Stoddard's *Review*, and two brief articles by the head girl of 1943/4, Ruth Hancock, and the head boy of the same year, Charles W. Pegg. This was done in conjunction with one of the reunion lunches, which had started in the early 1980s. In the same year, a service of 'celebration and thanksgiving' took place at All Saints, Marlpool, to commemorate the centenary. In the best traditions of school services, both priests at the service were old students (Kenneth Cupit and Stefan Krzeminski), as was the organist (John Reynolds). Needless to say, *He Who Would Valiant Be* featured in the service.

It was at one of the Heanorian reunions, in 2001, that the question of a 'school history' came up (again). As a result, those at the reunion were asked to send in any old memories of the school. While a history did not materialise at that time, the information did come in, and as a result of this the Old Students' Association started producing a biannual magazine of around 40 pages. The first edition was in March 2002. Not surprisingly, the title is '*The Heanorian*', now subtitled '*A Magazine for the Old Students of the Grammar School, Heanor*'. The magazine seeks to combine reminiscences of the School, with updates on what old students are now doing. Its circulation is now over 450 copies.

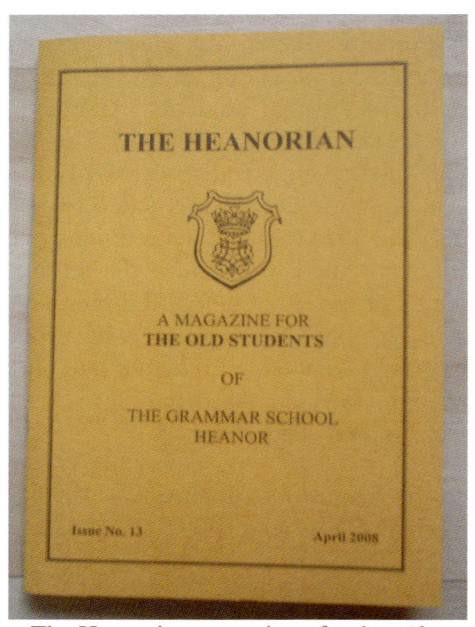

The Heanorian magazine of today, 'for Old Students of the Grammar School, Heanor'.

And so the story, and history, of Heanor Grammar School, is not yet over.

This history, like all histories, is incomplete. It does not tell the whole story, and cannot do so, as no one person has the whole story. If readers of this book know something which is not mentioned, then they can still share it with others. The Heanorians will be happy to hear from them, as will the Heanor and District Local History Society.

The story is not yet over. Not while there are any Old Students to remember!

> *... though he with giants fight,*
> *He will make good his right to be a pilgrim.*

Appendix

The Roll of Honour

Twice in this book, we have seen details of the memorials established to remember those pupils of Heanor Secondary School who died in either of the World Wars. There are few of their contemporaries now surviving, but it is incumbent upon us still to ensure that *'We Shall Remember Them'*.

1914 – 1918

L. Aldred	F. Kirk
N. Allen	G. Leivers
F. Amatt	P.E. Lockton
W. Annable	A. Martin
H.L. Baker	R. Martin
T.H. Beastall	W.E. Martin
M. Brown	A.G. Meads
G. Butt	G. Noon
W.S. Clarke	F.R. Oldershaw
T. Crumpton	G. Orrell
C. Dixon	W.H. Painter
C. Eyre	H.L. Parkin
G. Eyre	J.H. Parkin
R. Elleray	L. Parkin
A. Filsell	S. Raines
F.D. Fletcher	R. Roe
D. Fletcher	B. Rolling
H.C. Fletcher	C. Sadler
R. Foster	H. Saxton
F. Gardiner	H. Shooter
J. Holloway	C. Smalley
A. Holmes	R.C. Stoddard
B. Hudson	L.A. Stone
A.B. Hunt	F. Tilforth
J. Judge	F.O. Tucker
W. Judge	B. Warren
F. Keeling	N. Webster
T. Kerry	J.H. Wilson
	T. Walker

1939 – 1945

***In Memory of the Boys of our School who gave their lives
in the World War, 1939 – 1945***

G. Beckett	C.A. Newbold
R. Bolitho	J.E. Nicholson
L. Booth	A.A. Preston
E. Bradley	A.S. Pryor
H.A. Briggs	F. Richardson
J. Brown	E.E. Russell
R. Brown	F.L. Shears
D.W. Bunting	K.W. Shooter
J.L. Clarke	E. Taylor
M.W. Croft	J.H. Taylor
D. Flint	A. White
F.W.M.V. Fowler	L. Williams

Fideles usque ad mortem

The lectern containing the roll of honour from the 1939-45 War,
on the stage in front of the roll of honour forming part of
the Caley Robinson memorial to those who died in the 1914-18 War.

For further details of the Heanorian Magazine, please contact:
The Old Students' Association
Kimberley House
Church Lane
Morley
Derbyshire
DE7 6DE